GROUNDED

THE GROUNDED LEADER'S MANIFESTO

- Stay true to yourself.
- Be guided by your vision and your values, even when things feel chaotic and out of control.
- Stand courageously, with an open heart and strong back.
- Push the hair off your face and show up, even when it's uncomfortable.
- Stay curious.
- Be a fully human leader, embracing your unique strengths, imperfections and vulnerabilities.
- Believe. Stay focused and hopeful through adversity.
- Be a source of genuine, believable encouragement and support for others.
- Extend that same kindness and understanding to yourself.
- Align your words and actions with your values.
- Empower others to thrive, grow and bring their best.
- Foster environments of trust and encouragement.
- Champion inclusion by embracing diversity.
- Fiercely protect time to reflect.
- Celebrate your gains.
- Embrace the mantra 'Start over'.
- Spread hope! Inspire positive change in your team, organisation and the world.
- Prioritise your wellbeing with the same compassion you extend to others.
- Stand firm, stay human and lead with heart.

A note on the manifesto

I'm guessing you just read this manifesto and focused on what you're not doing well enough, or at all. But the manifesto is not a checklist or 'leadership style' to be perfected. I wrote it to inspire – to highlight and champion helpful, humble, powerful ways that we can be as humans and leaders.

Why don't you reread the manifesto, and acknowledge which of these calls to leadership you already do well?

Download a copy of the manifesto at **katrinabourke.com**.

KATRINA BOURKE

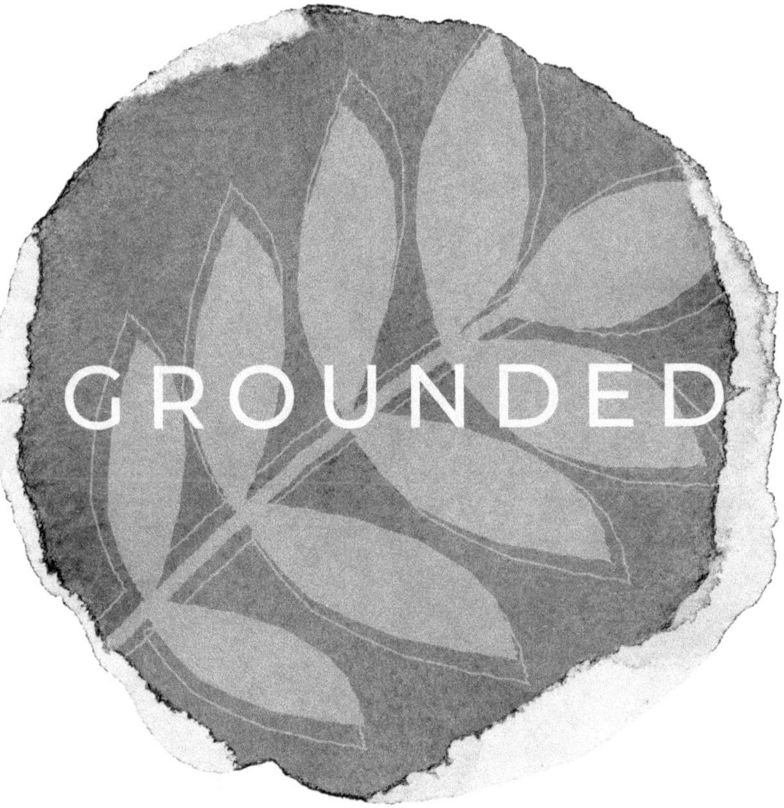

GROUNDED

A PRACTICAL PATH FOR CALM AND CONFIDENT LEADERSHIP

amba press

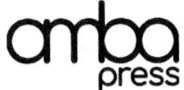

Published in 2025 by Amba Press, Melbourne, Australia
www.ambapress.com.au

© Katrina Bourke 2025

All rights reserved. No part of this book may be reproduced or transmitted in any form or by any means, electronic or mechanical, including photocopying, recording or by any information storage and retrieval system, without prior permission in writing from the publisher.

Cover design: Tess McCabe
Internal design: Amba Press
Editor: Brooke Lyons

ISBN: 9781923403185 (pbk)
ISBN: 9781923403192 (ebk)

A catalogue record for this book is available from the National Library of Australia.

Disclaimer: Pseudonyms are used for all case studies to protect privacy.

CONTENTS

Preface	ix
Author's Note: Oh the Irony	xi
Introduction: Push Your Hair off Your Face	1
Chapter One: Grounded	11
Chapter Two: Sacred Ground	15
Chapter Three: The Grounded Leadership Framework	37
Chapter Four: Decide	51
Chapter Five: Explore	71
Chapter Six: Honour	95
Chapter Seven: Lead	127
Conclusion	141
References	145
Acknowledgements	149
About the Author	153

PREFACE

Just before this book was submitted for editing, I suddenly and unexpectedly found myself in hospital. It was a frightening time. Initially doctors couldn't diagnose my sickness beyond 'infection' and I underwent a barrage of tests and examinations as they searched for the specific bacteria that were causing my fever and pain.

Thankfully all was revealed, and I was allowed to go home within a week. However, those days of lying in my hospital bed in feverish pain highlighted for me that the Grounded Leadership Framework – the model at the centre of this book – is not just for leaders: it can be a life raft in all sorts of uncertain and chaotic times for anyone who cares to use it.

In hospital, scared of possible complications and what the medical team might find, I became stressed. I began obsessing over what-ifs and shoulda, woulda, couldas. It took me a while, but eventually I realised that I was focusing on things beyond my control, giving away my power and getting stressed and obsessed over things that might never happen. I was adrift on a sea of worry, rocked by every new bit of information. My blood pressure was too high, my infection was not responding, nurses couldn't find a vein to insert the IV – all of it added to my fear and triggered stories in my mind of impending doom. I realised I was not helping myself by being so reactive. So I found my anchor: I decided how I wanted to 'do' my hospital stay. I wanted to focus on being grateful for the incredible care and access to high-quality science and medicine I had. I wanted to challenge myself to apply some of the practices in this book – to really live what I'm calling you to live – such as using my breath to remain calm and centred, focusing on what's within my control, setting a clear intention each day for how I want to be, and allowing but not indulging stories of doom and gloom.

I'm delighted to share that I am now fit and well, and fully recovered. But more than that: the experience reassured me that my Grounded Leadership Framework is fit for purpose! It's a solid map and guide for any human who wants to take control of how they show up in the world; for anyone who wants to be intentional and responsive to the trials, hiccups and blindsides that can occur at any given moment.

AUTHOR'S NOTE

OH THE IRONY

Back in 2018 I heard an interview with Dr Brené Brown, who was on tour at the time with her most recent book: *Dare to Lead*. (For the record, *Dare to Lead* is one of my most treasured books; my copy is overflowing with sticky notes, folded corners, highlighted paragraphs and underlined text.)

During the interview, Brown was discussing the process of writing her book and said something like, 'This book kicked my arse.' I was curious about that statement from her. It didn't make sense to me – I mean, she was in control, she was doing the writing – and I wondered what on earth she meant by it. At the time, I had no intention of writing my own book, but now, here I sit in the final throes of writing *Grounded* and I absolutely understand. It's taken me 12 months to put together this manuscript, but it contains a lifetime worth of lived experience, knowledge learned and wisdom gathered. It's built on my leadership experience, and that of many of my colleagues, friends and clients. It's a guide to helping you be a grounded leader, to align with your values and lead with authenticity and courage.

But to write it, I had to learn to truly live it – sometimes the hard way.

Back to the arse-kicking.

I did not see it coming. In fact, this book began in a picturesque Irish village, where I had the rare gift of time: two quiet months in the northern hemisphere winter of 2023–24. In the deep of an Irish cold snap, there isn't much to do as a tourist; so I gave myself permission to spend whole days inside. I gazed out at the rugged southern slopes of the Galtee Mountains, etched with silver streams – the Harps of Clieu – which appear after heavy rains or the thaw of snow. They're named for the mystical harper Clieu, who played to woo the daughter of a god said to dwell nearby.

The Galtees are steeped in folklore, their stories shifting with the ages. At different times, they were believed to be home to the fairy folk, a hunting ground for the legendary Finn MacCumhaill, a place of power and legend. Yet through every era, every mythology and every passing ruler, the mountains themselves have remained: silent, solid, enduring. And as I sat at their base, writing this book, they became a symbol of what it means to be grounded; to be deeply rooted in something that remains consistent and steadfast.

Once I landed back in Australia, I was busy with work, and the draft manuscript sat to the side and gathered dust until I decided to block out a week away and finalise it. I was keen, I was ready, I had a beautiful log cabin in the bush. I took my coffee machine, the dog and plenty of cake! The cabin was stacked with firewood and I was motivated to put the finishing touches to the book. I put out my stationery, my sticky notes, the large roll of baking paper I'd made use of to scribble and brainstorm on in Ireland. And then, I unpacked the long list of work-related tasks and reminders, many of them scribbled on sticky notes and random bits of paper: a colourful pile of all that I needed to attend to before I could focus on writing. I looked at the lists of calls to make, emails to write, follow-ups to plan and send. I saw the notes spilling out of my diary, stuffed into the pocket of my workbag, some clipped together and others now scattered across the cover of my manuscript… I saw all of this and I was frozen with overwhelm.

I cried.

I didn't know it at the time, but the arse-kicking had begun – and so had what I later came to call my 'log-cabin breakdown'.

As I look back now on one of my journal entries from that time, I feel so sad about how mean I was to myself while I was experiencing such pain and hurt. Rather than gifting myself the grace of understanding and compassion, I really stuck the knife in. I berated myself for not grinding on. In my journal I wrote:

> *I've woken up cranky, maybe even furious. I haven't touched the book! So typical of me. I haven't even gotten all my work done… What is wrong with me? Why?*

The irony of this experience was that I was writing a book on being grounded. I was writing about knowing your values, vision and intentions and bravely aligning to those things in order to stay grounded, stable and consistent when things get hectic. In workshops I help participants define and explore their strengths and the shadows that go with them. In coaching I support leaders to set goals, uncover habits, harness strengths, believe in themselves, treat themselves with patience and compassion and keep going.

And I was doing none of it.

I completely lost my shit. I spiralled down, blaming and shaming myself for not being focused, organised or dedicated enough to make the most of this time and get the job done.

Not only that, but I had taken on some advice about this book and how to write it – its direction and audience. Unfortunately that advice was just not right for me. Truth be told, I knew that at the time – I felt it in my gut as I was reworking the book, trying to fit it into the frame that my mentor had advised. And in another ironic, arse-kicking moment I became painfully aware that not only was the advice not right, but it also meant I now needed to rewrite large chunks of the book. Once again the irony was that I was writing a book about standing on your own sacred ground, staying aligned to your values and courageously trusting yourself. And once again, I was not taking my own advice.

When I returned to Melbourne a week later, I met with my mentor and therapist, Rose. She listened patiently, helpfully pointed out some blind spots and familiar patterns and kindly assisted me in reframing my 'log-cabin breakdown' into a 'bushland breakthrough'.

Whether it was a breakdown or a breakthrough, in my opinion this book is all the better for it. The book is stronger for the time it sat on the shelf while I put myself back together and reflected on the lessons of my experience. Some of the things I learned during that time have become essential elements of the sacred ground I now stand upon.

On the final day of my log-cabin stay I wrote the following entry in my journal:

> *This morning I notice my internal chatter saying something like, 'You've wasted your time here. You should have read more, written the book like you said you would,' and other such admonishments. But then I notice a smaller, kinder voice who says, 'You needed a rest. You made choices about other things you needed to do.' I will listen to that voice. I'm an adult. Imperfect, but a fully human adult who makes choices, doing the very best I can. I choose the kinder voice.*

JOURNAL PROMPTS

- Right now, at the beginning of this journey, what is resonating with you about what you have read so far?
- What are you searching for in reading this book and engaging with its messages?
- Which internal voice is driving you? The harsh, critical, admonishing voice or a smaller, kinder voice?

INTRODUCTION

PUSH YOUR HAIR OFF YOUR FACE

My nana was a CWA lady – a member of the Country Women's Association. The CWA are renowned in Australia for their baking (among many other skills) and Nana did her bit to uphold that legend. Her afternoon teas were epic: the lightest and tallest sponge cakes you've ever seen always stood proudly at the centre of the table, surrounded by biscuits, jellies, madeleines, slices, tarts, cupcakes and, finally, dainty finger sandwiches (to balance out all the sugar!).

Once I became a teenager, I was deemed old enough to be allowed to help Nana set the table and lay out all the dishes in preparation for visitors who were coming to tea. At the time, I was uncomfortable in my body. I had spotty skin and endless self-doubt and I found it difficult to take my seat at many of the tables I might have rightly belonged at. At Nana's table, she, who was always so proud and supportive of me, would look at me with my fringe of dark hair hanging in my eyes and say, 'Push your hair off your face, dear. Let us see you.' In true teenage style, I would roll my eyes and hunch down a little deeper into myself.

I spent many years hunched down into myself: keeping quiet, trying to stay under the radar, convinced I was a weirdo who never quite fitted in. And of course, the more I believed this version of myself, the more evidence I found that supported it. I'd pop my head up, speak up or stand out in some way and it would often go poorly – like the time I entered a public speaking competition in my later teens. Presenting my prepared speech went well, but when I had to improvise at the end to answer the judges' questions I felt tongue-tied and worried about what they would think of my responses – were they 'right'? I used humour to keep the answers light and funny, staying away from anything deeper, refraining from sharing what I really thought. The judges laughed, but I didn't win the competition. I added that 'loss' to my collection of evidence supporting my belief that I wasn't good enough, there were always others who were better and, anyway, who did I think I was to be speaking up and putting myself out there like that?

My heart aches for teenage me. I wish she could have seen and heard and believed the encouraging moments and people that surrounded her – for there were many.

It took me a long while to learn to see and believe the positive. In fact, it's still a work in progress!

One moment of insight from my journalling reminds me of the ongoing nature of self-awareness and self-compassion:

> *I can shed my stories of 'not enough', but it's not a one-shed and it's done. Rather, it's like a snake with its skin – re-shedding it over and again. It's seasonal perhaps. But not four seasons spread neatly over the year, more like four in a day or sometimes even four in an hour!*

As an adult I became a school leader – a deputy principal for many years – and I prided myself on being the go-to person in the school. If there was a question to be answered, a problem to be solved, a crisis to tackle, a situation to defuse, I was the one to ask. I loved the adrenaline of that, and I loved the importance of being at the centre of everything – a strange place for an introvert to love being, but it made me feel important and necessary and like I was contributing. People would congratulate me on how calm I was, how confident and courageous I was. I would smile and nod and dismiss their compliments, while at the same time feeling secretly pleased that that was what they saw – because on the inside it was a very different story. I was a mess! I was the proverbial duck on the surface – looking cool and calm and confident, but paddling furiously under the water to keep up appearances; to keep up with all I felt I should be doing.

It turns out that paddling furiously, trying to be perfect and be all things to all people, is not a sustainable strategy. In fact, it turns out that keeping up the above-water facade of calm is a classic tactic to escape that nagging feeling that you're somehow 'not enough'.

The problem is that eventually the above-water facade begins to crack. Imperfections start to leak through. And sure enough, that's what happened to me. I began to drop the ball here and there, I forgot things, I missed deadlines and made mistakes. I started to feel like I wasn't cut out for the job anymore. I wondered what had gone wrong. What was I not doing well enough? I desperately wanted someone to come into work and watch me do my thing and tell me what to do to fix the problems I was experiencing. I'm not sure that such a person existed and I certainly didn't have time to find out. So I doubled down. I worked harder and longer; I dialled up the external facade. I didn't want anyone to see that I was making mistakes or needed help – for me, at the time, that would have been the worst possible outcome.

And that was just at work – I'm not even mentioning my personal life. The ones I loved the most got the leftovers of me. They were fitted into the cracks of my days. I felt bad, I felt terrible, but again, I didn't know how to fix it, so again, I doubled down. I did all I could for them. If they asked me to attend something or help with something, I was there. I didn't want them to think they didn't matter. I didn't want to give them reasons to complain about my job and I didn't want to have to say no. I tried to do all the things I thought a good partner, sister, daughter and friend should.

By the time I decided to leave my job, I was resentful, exhausted and burned out. I didn't know that then, of course; I thought I was a failure, and that my circumstances (and some of the people around me) were to blame.

I know I'm not alone in this. So many leaders, especially leaders in education, find themselves in a similar spot – trying to hold it all together while paddling furiously below the surface. This book is for you.

What I couldn't see then was that the answer wasn't to double down or work harder. These are both forms of running away from the discomfort of the internal critic. A better solution would have been to pause and lean on my sacred ground: the parts of me that could bolster my self-belief and help me to see that I *was* enough and was *doing* enough. If I knew then what I know now, I could have allowed my sacred ground to hold me steady and provide the self-compassion I needed to continue to lead.

Over time, Nana's encouragement to push my hair off my face and let people see me has resurfaced, and I've become intentional about doing just that. But it hasn't just happened. I have intentionally built a solid, strong, safe foundation that anchors me – my sacred ground. I step onto it with intention and allow my sacred ground to anchor and hold me. I let people see and hear me, even when my voice shakes.

This book is my way of paying forward Nana's wisdom to you, leader – to help you create your own sacred ground so that you can stand up and speak up, and let the world – or at least *your* world – see and hear you and benefit from your unique wisdom.

Education is a human-centred profession – even though, in an age of increasing centralisation, bureaucracy and AI, it may not feel that way at times. But as educators, we work with humans and we serve humans – be they students, families or colleagues. Our most influential work is with young humans, supporting and growing them into adults who make a positive impact in the world.

We need human-centred leaders to navigate and lead that work. We need human leaders who have experienced the vulnerabilities and frailties as well as the adulations and joys of being fully human. We need leaders who've experienced those highs and lows – and the bits in between – and who, rather than running away from it, can draw on that experience to understand, empathise and connect with other humans who are having their own experience.

In his online space *The AI Educator*, Dan Fitzpatrick recently wrote of a 'liminal space… a transitional phase where old norms are losing meaning and a new way hasn't been fully formed yet' (Fitzpatrick, 2024). Leader, I believe this is *our* time and space. The time is ripe; the need is there for human-centred, imperfect, vulnerable, courageous, humble and authentic humans to help form that new way, especially in schools. We need leaders who have solid guiding foundations yet remain flexible in how they show up. Leaders who have clear boundaries and uphold them, yet forgive their own and others' trespasses across those boundaries. Leaders who are unapologetically of service to and compassionate towards others and who also deem themselves worthy of receiving both of those gifts. Leaders who see their purpose as making things happen, making things better. Leaders who know they can't do it on their own and that, in fact, together with others is better.

Imperfection and vulnerability are just two elements of what it means to be human, but in my experience, they punch above their weight in terms of the headspace they take up. And who better to see and understand the myriad ways that human vulnerabilities show up in people than another human who has their own lived experience of vulnerability. That's you, isn't it? You have the experience of being a human, of the doubts and frailties that come with that, and the quiet, persistent voice of courage that speaks to you and won't allow you to hunch down and stay down.

This book will help you to get grounded. It will offer you insights, suggestions, stories, strategies and practical steps that you can use to map and strengthen your sacred ground. In the chapters that follow we'll be guided by my Grounded Leadership Framework. I'll offer you opportunities, tools and evidence-based research that will help you to 'Understand and lead yourself in order to understand and lead others' (Hougaard & Carter, 2018).

Throughout this book, you'll be invited to:

- **Decide** on the leader you aspire to be
- **Explore** the human you are
- **Honour** the practices that help you show up
- **Lead** the way to positive change.

> **JOURNAL PROMPTS**
>
> Imagine you were to push the hair off your face and bravely step forward.
>
> - What might you say that you're currently not saying?
> - What might you do that you're currently not doing?

An invitation and a challenge

Not far from where I live in Melbourne lies Hanging Rock, known to some of its traditional owners as Ngannelong. It's sacred ground for many First Nations peoples who for centuries used it as a space to gather, hold ceremonies, conduct business, and trade.

Quite near to Hanging Rock is a place that has become sacred to me: Mt Macedon. This patch of rugged native bush became my sacred place during the time when my mum was dying. It was hard. Bloody hard. To help me navigate that hard stuff and show up for Mum as I wanted to, I would go each day to ground myself with a walk among the trees and up and down the hills.

It was there in the bush that I tapped into the calming energy of nature – my favourite way to get grounded.

I got to know the kookaburra who would fly in as I arrived early each morning and flit from tree to tree, following me like a sentry until I entered the bush. I learned to appreciate the spooky darkness of the ferny glen at the bottom of the hill. I loved padding silently on the pine needles in the tiny patch of pine forest. I learned to listen for the quiet call of the owl, each 'Hoo' perfectly spaced from the next. I always heard her in one particular spot on the mountain, never anywhere else. I knew she was there and yet I never saw her.

Some days I would sit and marvel at the crystal-clear reflections of the trees in the still waters of the lake. On other days my path would take me deep into the bush, and I would find myself standing at the foot of one of the biggest trees on the mountain, ancient, scarred and still firmly rooted in the ground.

Here and there throughout the forest were flashes of vegetation that didn't quite seem to belong – remnant species from when a plant nursery had stood on the site. They were European trees; deciduous and 'not quite right' in the Australian landscape, but at the same time responsible for some of the most vibrant colour and lovely, scenic spots throughout the bush.

My favourite time in that part of the bush is in autumn, when an incredible array of fungi is there to discover. Walking through the dark glades I spy the brilliant blues of *Mycena interrupta*, the delicate shell-like pinks of *Scytinotus longinquus* and the fairytale red-and-white spots of *Amanita muscaria*.

The fungi we see popping up on logs and in paddocks and any number of other places are called the 'fruiting bodies'. These fruiting bodies are exciting to spot, but they become even more special when you learn that they are really just a hint of the incredible underground network – called mycelium – that is mostly hidden to the naked eye. Science has discovered that mycelium is crucial to the survival and health of the trees, plants and grasses of the bush as it connects, nourishes and informs them all.

It's often in autumn that the fruiting bodies emerge, and even then only when the conditions are just right. Take, for example, the bioluminescent ghost fungus (*Omphalotus nidiformis*) which appears across Australian forests in late autumn and winter. It fruits only when the air is damp and the temperatures drop. Too dry, and it won't emerge. Too cold, and its eerie glow fades.

As you read this book I invite you to be alert to what is waiting to emerge from within you. Working through the journal prompts will, I hope, help you to tap into the incredible network of gifts, strengths, habits, wisdom and experience that are within you already, just waiting for the right conditions to emerge.

I want you to gain a sense of affirmation from this book: that you are enough as you are right now.

I want you to be inspired to bravely put yourself out there and lead, with quiet confidence in your value and ability.

I want you to get clearer on the leader you want to be, and what is required in order for you to achieve that.

And finally, as you read, I dearly hope that you'll write notes in the margins, underline bits that you love, sticky-note the pages you want to come back to, fold the corners over and write into your journal the phrases and sentences that are meaningful to you.

This book issues you an invitation and a challenge: map and build your sacred ground; it's important work. But don't just build it – you must also tend it, maintain it, renovate it, reinforce it and, most importantly of all: apply it.

Now more than ever we need grounded, courageous, clear and compassionate leaders. In a world where it's all too easy to be cancelled or to offend, we need leaders who can courageously speak up and act with integrity, who can be vulnerably human in the pursuit of making a meaningful difference.

JOURNAL PROMPTS

I've shared with you what I want for you from this book, but what really matters is:

- What do you want?
- What are you hoping to gain from this book?
- What is already stirring within you and waiting to emerge?

CHAPTER ONE

GROUNDED

*A day is precious because each day is essentially
the microcosm of your whole life.*

John O'Donohue

As a small child I would walk with my grandfather through the bush surrounding his home in the Plenty Ranges, just north of Melbourne. As each season came and went he would point out how the landscape and the animal life would act and adapt according to the weather. I felt the briskness of winter, appreciated the shade from the tall trees in summer and was always delighted to see the green shoots that signalled spring was coming, and, later, the brilliant orange hues of the sunrises and the drying leaves that signalled the falling of autumn.

Then, during my teenage years, I lived in the Mallee, a remote region in the north-west of Victoria. I don't remember four seasons there, although that is most likely due to the fact that I was a teenager and was much less focused on the natural world around me, caught up instead in the usual adolescent anxiety to blend in with my peers and be less awkward.

The Mallee is deep dusty desert, saltbush, red earth, bindii weeds, dust storms, hot summers and freezing-cold winter mornings. Water is precious. Earth is all around; even inside, where the red dust relentlessly accumulates on any flat surface.

I have been connected to and aware of the ground I have stood on since very early childhood. And yet the image that comes most strongly to mind when I think of being *grounded* is not the earth at all. It's water: the tides and waves of the ocean.

Have you ever looked out from the beach and noticed the bright yellows, reds and greens of the navigation buoys bobbing around in the water? These towers are signposts and guides for those navigating watercraft through the invisible lanes and pathways of the seas.

Often the navigation buoys sway slightly with the gentle rhythm of the water, while at other times they might get rocked violently, smashed by the waves and wind. Whatever the surrounding weather, though, a navigation buoy always returns to upright. That's thanks to its ballast – the steadying weight that keeps the whole thing stable and afloat. In addition to the ballast, navigation buoys have anchors that lie deep below, keeping them in place and stopping them from being washed far away at the mercy of the waves.

The ballast (the steadying weight) and the anchor (the place-keeper) are essential to staying grounded. Our sacred ground is our unique personal combination of the things that anchor us and at the same time keep us buoyant; the vision, the values, the practices that allow us to lead with courage and compassion, to be well, to show up as the leader we aspire to be and to do good work.

The Spinning Principal

Let me tell you the story of the Spinning Principal. We'll call him Joseph – he deserves a name for he is, after all, one of the inspirations for this book. Joseph is one of my coaching clients. On the particular day this anecdote was born, I had travelled to his school for our coaching session. He has a very nice office – it's situated right in the centre of the school and features an entire wall of glass looking out over the schoolyard, and a couple of comfy lounge chairs. I was sitting on one of those chairs, waiting for Joseph to arrive. Thanks to the glass wall, I was able to watch him make his way across the yard and down the hallway towards his office.

As I watched him weave through playing children and duck flying basketballs, I observed a school-based version of the arcade game Whac-a-Mole begin to unfold. I noticed a staff member approach him and grab his attention in conversation for a few minutes. Joe then proceeded towards his office, until very quickly another staff member appeared, engaging him in conversation for a quick moment. With that conversation concluded, Joseph started walking towards his office again when a third staff member appeared – seemingly out of nowhere – and requested his attention.

By the time Joseph got to his office and stepped inside the door, it seemed to me that his eyes were spinning in his head. In fact, his whole body seemed to be spinning ever so slightly! I watched this and wondered how on earth we were going to have a useful, impactful coaching conversation.

There was (and is) nothing wrong with Joseph. He's not a poor leader or a poor communicator or a poor manager of his time and boundaries. In fact, I know him to be quite good at all of those things.

Spinning – that feeling of being bombarded and pulled in every direction, like everyone wants a piece of you – is widespread, and most definitely endemic to our schools and school system.

As humans and as leaders, we spin a lot of plates, but that doesn't mean we have to get sucked into the vortex that the spinning creates. Getting grounded is the antidote to spinning. It's the way we anchor ourselves within it. This is where quality leaders focus their energy – on being grounded, on staying anchored and remaining buoyant, rather than railing against the spinning.

Even the most grounded of leaders gets knocked off-kilter from time to time and gets sucked into the spinning. That's exactly what happened to Joseph on the day I came to visit him. But Joseph is a grounded leader. He has terrific tools and strategies and intentions that help him to stay grounded and to return to his own sacred ground when he finds himself adrift. And on that day, Joseph, the Spinning Principal, was able to right himself using one of the tools we had practised. I watched him take a deep breath and physically and mentally ground himself before pushing the hair off his face and stepping forward once more, ready, present and eager to engage in our coaching conversation.

> **GROUNDED LEADERSHIP PRACTICE**
>
> Want to try the same strategy that Joseph the Spinning Principal used? Try the Look Down, Slow Down, Narrow Down technique:
>
> - **Look down:** Start where your feet are, notice and become present.
> - **Slow down:** Breathe out: a long, slow exhale.
> - **Narrow down:** Identify one next step. Then push the hair off your face and step forward.

CHAPTER TWO

SACRED GROUND

*Slow down and approach your inner landscape
with courage and curiosity.*

Susan David

Your sacred ground is your unique and personally crafted combination of the things that anchor you, sustain you and allow you to lead with courage and compassion; to be well, to show up as the leader you aspire to be and to do good work.

Hanging Rock, the sacred place I mentioned in the introduction to this book, is known in geological terms as a mamelon rock formation. Mamelons are formed from lava, but rather than being the result of a spectacular volcanic eruption, they are created by lava forming mounds as it pushes through the earth. Over time new mounds layer upon the existing ones, eventually forming unique and fascinating structures, some of impressive height.

Just as mamelon rocks are formed over time, layer upon layer, from the cooling remains of lava, so too is our sacred ground formed and strengthened by our experiences – the joyful and the painful – our values, our environment and many other factors that form the sand, silt, rock and grit of how we live and lead.

Mapping, navigating, exploring and developing the layers of our sacred ground is a work in progress. It's not something we charge at, work hard on and then it's done, allowing us to finally get started on leading. Nope. The fun, the vulnerability and the daring required to form sacred ground is what Simon Sinek might call an 'infinite game': a game that never ends, where we learn as we go and no-one is ever crowned the winner.

Many of us feel uncomfortable with the fact that the layering of sacred ground takes time. We like to tick things off, get shit done, be efficient, get ahead. As educators who are time-poor and task-heavy, getting through our days depends on our ability to get things done, and fast.

Participants in my workshops, where we explore, map and craft our sacred ground, often feel discomfort and frustration, especially in the early stages of our work together (that's probably not a great advertisement for my work!). I create space for them to slow down and encourage them to stay there: to be slower, to reflect, consider and contemplate – things they just don't have time for in the daily life of a school. I remember one participant in particular: Jessie. Highly competent, intelligent and a voracious learner, she was initially frustrated in the work. She was quick to finish each exercise and keen to move on to the next thing. About halfway through our 12-month project Jessie expressed out loud with wonder – and a wry, self-aware laugh – her realisation that the exploring, reflecting, connecting, mapping and discovering we do *is* the work. It *is* the goal. It *is* the outcome.

Our sacred ground is a coming together of who we are, what we've done, why we are, what we want to do and achieve, how we honour ourselves and how we show up. We bring these pieces together by doing the work of my Grounded Leadership Framework: *Deciding, Exploring, Honouring* and *Leading*.

It's not a quick job. We add layers as we deepen our understanding, refine our practices, tease out nuance, clarify our purpose, and collaborate with, challenge and empower others.

This work requires time to unfold – two kinds of time. It takes kairos time: those expansive, unmeasured moments where things settle and what is waiting more deeply below has space to surface. Kairos time is where we have space to wander, expand and reflect, consider possibilities, reconnect and realign. There's no diary, no time pressure, no deadline. It's where insight and inspiration live.

And then there's chronos time: our calendars, our clocks, our meetings and Monday mornings. Chronos time is where we show up, take action and apply our insights.

John O'Donohue wrote about curved and linear paths: 'The imagination in its loyalty to possibility, often takes the curved path rather than the linear way' (O'Donohue, 1997). His curved path reminds me of kairos time – spacious, unmeasured, intuitive. The kind of time that invites us to soften, to listen, to let things flow. The linear path speaks more to chronos time – focused, structured, moving us forward with intention.

Grounded leadership calls us to walk both paths, to move intelligently and intentionally between kairos and chronos. Without kairos, we move fast but stay shallow. Without chronos, we stay in the world of imagination and fail to build anything solid.

Unfortunately in our present day where demands are high and time is scarce, the linear path is alluring and can seem the obvious choice. It's faster, quicker, more efficient. But part of evolving as a grounded leader and mapping our sacred ground is allowing time to wander the curved path of space, wonder and possibility. Along the curved path, layers and layers will form, adding ballast, strength and conviction to who we are and how we show up in the world. Our sacred ground then becomes not just something we build, but something we can rely on to uphold and support us as we go about the complex work of being the leader and human we aspire to be.

Earlier I shared with you how, when I think of leadership sacred ground, one of the images that comes to mind is of brightly coloured navigation buoys that guide and direct water traffic. The buoys bob on the surface of the water, kept buoyant by their ballast and held in place by their anchor. Your sacred ground is the ballast that keeps you buoyant *and* it's the anchor that holds you in place. Your sacred ground is unique to you. It's a reflection of your inner world and the unique collection of stories, experiences, strategies, values, strengths, shadows, goals and habits that have layered over time and now influence how you show up. Your sacred ground also supports you to courageously show up as your authentic self.

When the spaces we live and work in are reasonably calm, we might not even notice our sacred ground. But when the wind and the waves whip up and things start to get complex and messy, our sacred ground is crucial. It's what allows us to stay grounded and navigate our way through chaos and complexity as the leader and human we aspire to be.

Of course, sacred ground is metaphorical. It's not real ground at all, rather it's the combination of things that make you *you*. They are all very real. And like real ground, they can form a strong foundation allowing you to plant your feet, push the hair off your face, declare your intent and maintain your balance as you do the work of showing up and leading with grounded confidence.

Sacred ground gives us double bang-for-our-buck. By learning about our layers, we come to understand ourselves and how and why we function the way we do. With this knowledge we are empowered and we develop grounded confidence. We develop self-worth and self-belief that strengthen us, and embolden us to show up aligned to our values and our vision. Eventually, and more and more often, our sacred ground becomes what drives and propels us into action, replacing the old drivers of fear, of 'should' and of worry about what others will think or whether we are doing it 'right'.

Sacred ground is something we explore and refine and get to know well, and in doing so it becomes not just a reflection of who we are but also a means of grounding us and giving us courage to be who we are.

Brené Brown says, 'Who we are is how we lead' (Brown, 2018). Our sacred ground is who we are.

On sacredness

My mum would not be offended to hear me describe her as a genuine hippie. I have a great photo of her, taken when she visited San Francisco, standing on the stairs at 710 Ashbury Street – the same stairs that Jerry Garcia and the Grateful Dead fooled around on in what became an iconic image for *Rolling Stone* magazine. For my mum, and for many Deadheads, those stairs, that space, is sacred.

Many years ago, on my own overseas travels, I was browsing in an Irish bookshop and came across *The Traveller's Guide to Sacred Ireland*. Over the years I have been fortunate to use that book to guide my travels throughout Ireland, visiting an abundance of ruins, ancient stone carvings and holy wells – many of which were considered sacred by the ancient Celts and other pre-Christian traditions. With the spread of Christianity their significance was recognised or, perhaps, reinterpreted, ensuring their preservation as sacred Christian sites.

Whether it's the front stairs of the Grateful Dead house in San Francisco or the natural wells and stone carvings of Ireland, each sacred space is assigned that status because, for the communities it is attached to, it is for some reason 'extremely important and deserving respect' (*Cambridge Dictionary*).

If you are to have an impact on this world and make the difference you wish to make, it's important to believe that your sacred ground is extremely important and deserving of respect.

This does not require you to start strutting around like a proud peacock proclaiming how extremely important you are. In fact, I suspect that you can think of a peacock-like leader or two who you would most definitely not like to emulate. Rather, mapping your sacred ground is about developing a deep understanding and awareness of yourself, what you stand for and what helps you to be the best version of yourself. The Grounded Leadership Framework is designed to help you do this: to define your vision, to deepen your self-awareness and to compile a personalised collection of practices, tools and strategies that support you to be your best and lead with impact.

Being a leader requires courage and stamina. To maintain a supply of both of these qualities you have to care for and nurture yourself and your sacred ground. If you don't see yourself and your sacred ground as important and deserving of respect, how will you do the work of sustaining and nurturing yourself? And how will others see you as someone with something important to say and a vision worth getting on board with?

Sacred ground as a source of strength

My ears always prick up when I hear clients talk about sacred ground. I've learned that they conjure those words when they want to describe their commitment and desire to be themselves and stay true to that. They use the term to conjure their strength and their power. Not power over anyone or anything else; rather, power from within – the courage and strength to navigate their day or a particular situation while staying true to themselves.

When I'm with a client discussing a challenge and how they might handle it, often, at the end of our session as they are preparing to go forth and take action, they say to me, 'I just need to stay on my sacred ground.' What they mean is they need to trust themselves: trust that they know what they know, trust that their experience, wisdom and courage will get them through. All of those things form sacred ground, and together they provide the ballast that anchors my clients and gives them the strength to dare to believe that they can successfully navigate what is ahead.

Values

Jonah is a school leader I've had the privilege of working with for many years. He has always been dedicated to exploring the layers of his sacred ground, piecing together the values, experiences and shadows that help him make sense of why he feels more strongly about some things than others, and why he finds it easier to be himself in some situations than others.

One afternoon Jonah called me, and told me he'd had a pretty tough afternoon. His employer was bringing in new administration systems and processes and new personnel to run them. As a result, some existing positions would be made redundant, and Jonah had been instructed to fire a long-standing member of the administration team. Jonah was furious. He felt sick about having to fire a colleague. He had been wracking his brain all afternoon for ways to save him.

As we talked, it became clear to Jonah that his anger at his employer and his desire to refuse to follow instructions were rooted in his values of fairness and compassion. He didn't believe it was fair or just to sack a staff member of long-standing service and loyalty, and he didn't feel his employer was giving any deference to that. Jonah was being knocked off-kilter, and the very things that ordinarily helped to anchor him and guide how he chose to show up – his values of fairness and compassion – were crashing into his employer's directive.

Jonah was tearing his hair out when we spoke because he simply could not imagine, and would not consider, going against his values. He didn't see how it was possible to do so and be his authentic self.

In the end, Jonah found a way. He talked openly to the employee. He negotiated an exit timeline that was helpful to his staff member, and that his employer was willing to go along with. Importantly, he looked back at the situation and was able to hold his head high. He had acted in alignment with his values; he'd been fair and transparent with his employee and employer. In Jonah's words, he had been able to do this by intentionally standing on his sacred ground.

Jonah's story is a great example of being anchored by sacred ground. His values were the anchor that steadied him and the motivation for his actions. Other layers of his sacred ground were in play, too: emotional intelligence, self-awareness and the practical, solution-focused communication skills he had developed. All of these gave him the confidence to believe in himself, the conviction to back himself and the courage to speak up with grounded confidence, even though his voice shook.

My Grounded Leadership Framework will help you to explore and define your values and vision. One of the fruits of that work is grounded confidence – the kind of deep knowing that gives you the courage to show up and lead with conviction.

Knowing your values and understanding how they deeply represent and guide you, along with being clear on your vision for yourself as a leader, will empower and embolden you to lead with grounded confidence.

It's worth slowing down here to consider that word 'embolden'. I chose it deliberately. The *Collins English Dictionary* defines 'Bold' as:

1. *Courageous, confident, and fearless, ready to take risks.*
2. *Showing or requiring courage.*

It *is* bold to lead. It *is* bold to put your words and ideas out there for others to scrutinise and consider. Maybe they'll agree with or add value to your offerings, but there's also the possibility that others will disagree, attack or mock you or your ideas. And that's where vulnerability comes in.

Vulnerability

Brené Brown (2012) describes vulnerability as 'uncertainty, risk and emotional exposure'. She gives us what I consider a stark, but somehow comforting, truth: 'There is no courage without vulnerability.'

If vision and values are the *what* of grounded leadership, vulnerability is the *how*. Leading from our values, pursuing our vision and inviting – even imploring – others to join us in that pursuit: that's courageous. And that's vulnerability.

As a leader, there's the very real and very vulnerable possibility that people will disagree with you. Your vision and your values are yours. They're not necessarily shared by others. Others also have their own visions and values which they hold and aspire to just as passionately as you hold yours. As humans, with brains that are in service of keeping us safe and connected to other humans, we don't love the idea that other humans may actively disagree with us. In fact, it sets off physiological alarm bells.

There's another dimension of vulnerability, too: knowing that even though your values are deeply held and might even seem to be who you are, at times they might not be enough. This is perhaps one of the hardest leadership lessons of all: sometimes, even when we act in full alignment with our values, we are still left with an imperfect outcome.

In the example of Jonah, staying true to his values of fairness and compassion gave him the grounded confidence to advocate for his staff member and ultimately to negotiate an exit date for him that seemed fair. But perhaps the ultimate expression of Jonah's fairness value would have been if the person had not been dismissed at all. Was it fair that just because his employer was implementing new systems a staff member had to go? Jonah got to walk away with his head held high because he acted in alignment with his values and did all he could – but in the end, the dismissal of the staff member still happened, and it was beyond Jonah's control to stop it.

Jonah's story is just one example of how values, when tested by reality, can lead to complex, difficult situations. And this tension is not unique – leaders everywhere face moments where their values are challenged by circumstance. Take, for example, a recent conversation I had with a network of school principals about grounded leadership in the context of the very real challenges they face as principal leaders.

One principal stood up to share what was unsettling her – how a looming staff shortage was forcing her to confront a difficult compromise. With the start of the school year approaching, she was facing a stark reality: there simply weren't enough teachers to ensure every class had one. One of her core values was excellence and she was accustomed to using this as a filter to guide her decisions. Yet, given the shortage of quality applicants, she knew she might have to appoint at least one teacher who didn't fully meet that standard. 'How do I align with that?' she asked.

It turned out to be a passionate discussion. Another leader, whose leadership team also upheld excellence as a core value, was almost vehement in her response: 'There is no compromise. It's not negotiable. It's excellence – or we find another way until we can find excellence.'

But not everyone agreed. Others in the room felt that the greater responsibility was to ensure that every class had a teacher – even if they weren't ideal – and then work out the details from there.

The range of opinions reflected the range of values in the room – all deeply held and sometimes in direct conflict. And this is the work of leadership: standing firm in our values while holding space for the discomfort of disagreement.

JOURNAL PROMPTS

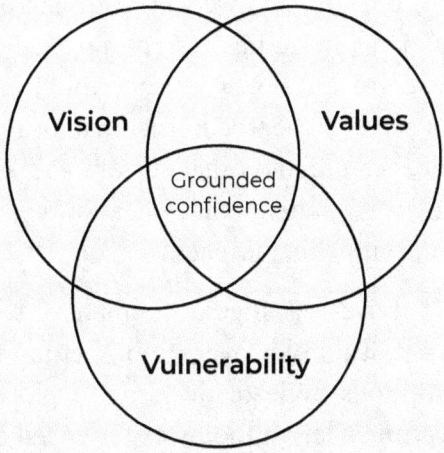

I invite you to take the Venn diagram above and explore it in regard to you as a leader. What comes up for you in each of the circles? Consider the following prompts:

- What is your vision for yourself as leader? What do you see as the impact and difference you want to make?
- What are some of the values that guide you?
- What is your relationship with vulnerability?

One of my mentors, Matt, always says that the really interesting parts of a Venn diagram are in the overlaps, so I encourage you to take the time to discover what is waiting to emerge for you in the spaces that overlap. You might like to consider:

- What are some of the opportunities that emerge when vision and vulnerability come together?
- What is the product of vulnerability and values?
- When vision and values combine, what occurs? What is challenged or quashed?

Clarity

One outcome of doing the work of the Grounded Leadership Framework is greater clarity. As we work through each stage of the framework – exploring, reflecting, reframing, deepening –you'll get clearer on who you are and how you lead. You'll get greater clarity on the leader you aspire to be, the human habits and strengths you bring to your role, the practices that sustain and support you and the skills, tools and ways of being that will allow you to lead in a way that has a positive, compelling impact.

But clarity doesn't arrive as a singular moment of certainty. Instead, like leadership itself, it unfolds over time. 'Getting grounded' is an evolution; a continuous cycle of deciding, exploring, honouring, leading and reflecting. Clarity, too, is experienced as an evolution. It's an outcome of the Grounded Leadership Framework, but it's not an end result. You'll get clear, then you'll be less clear, you'll get clear and then you'll land in confusion once more – even chaos at times.

But rest assured, chaos in this context is not to be feared. While chaos is not something we typically look forward to or seek out – writer Margaret Wheatley even goes so far as to claim 'it's always unsettling, discouraging and depressing' – chaos can be 'life's process for transformation and growth'. Wheatley concludes 'it's the only route to profound change' (Wheatley, 2023).

The cycle, from confusion to clarity and round about and back again, will give you a resonance, a depth of knowing and a certain tenor to your voice. This is grounded confidence – you'll speak up, push the hair off your face and contribute even when your voice shakes, because you are deeply called to do so.

Wheatley (2023) eloquently sums up the relationship between chaos, clarity and the mapping of our sacred ground as leaders when she says:

> The Chaos Cycle doesn't end in chaos. It ends with heightened clarity and inspired meaning for how we can use our power

and influence to serve this time. We can trust this path – it leads us out of the dark woods into a bright clearing where we realise what is truly meaningful in our lives and work.

Perhaps right now you're wondering if this is a selfish pursuit; if all this courage and confidence will go to your head and turn you into the sort of cocky leader you are usually repelled by.

Fear not. I'm encouraging you to pursue clarity as an act of service. As a leader, *your* energy, *your* clarity, *your* courage and *your* confidence radiate out to those you serve.

Your clarity matters. As a member and leader of a team, your clarity – of thought and purpose and articulation – instils confidence. It inspires and encourages others to step into their leadership.

Figure 2.1: Ripples of clarity

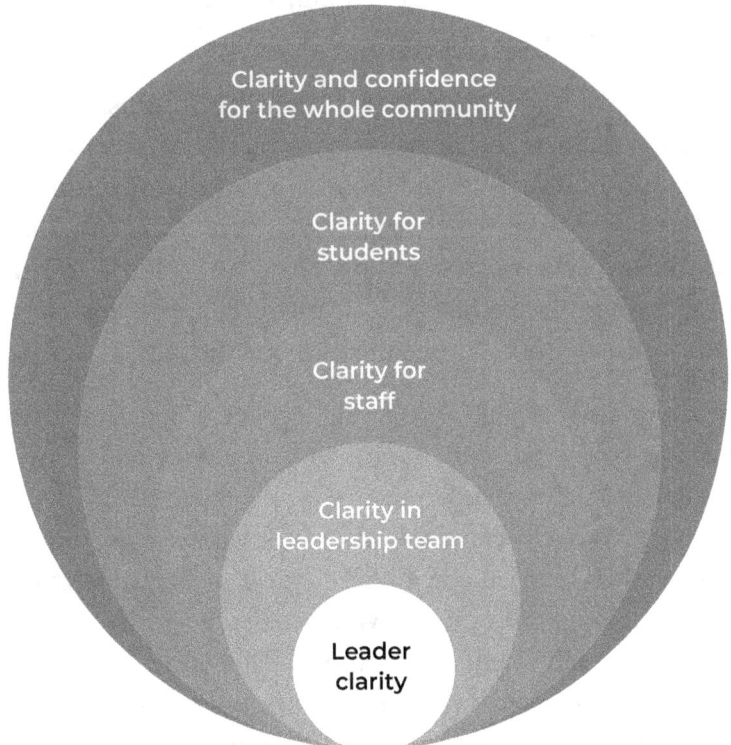

As figure 2.1 shows, clarity ripples out to the entire school ecosystem. A leadership team that values and operates with clarity creates a climate where staff feel confident that their leaders' messaging and actions are clearly articulated and consistently applied. Students also benefit as they learn, grow and play in a climate where expectations and conditions are clear and consistent. Clarity and consistency of approach and expectations from the school build credibility across the entire community.

Clarity and integrity are closely linked. When what we say and what we do are aligned, we build trust. When they're misaligned, we create the conditions for confusion, contradiction or conflict to take hold.

Because of the pressure to do so much coupled with the finite amount of time available, 'problems often arise from unquestioned assumptions and deeply habitual ways of acting' (Senge et al., 2004). This is despite our best intentions and our knowledge of change management best practices.

My Integrity Matrix tool, shown in figure 2.2, helps leaders and teams uncover their assumptions and habits and consider how these are impacting clarity and culture. It helps you see the culture you have versus the culture you *think* you're creating. The Integrity Matrix serves as a mirror during change, implementation and evaluation where individuals and teams can check: Are we clear? Are we consistent? What conditions are we creating?

To use the matrix, begin by selecting a process, a routine or a way of working you're part of. It could be how you and your team communicate in meetings, or your school's expectations for report writing. Ask yourself: Have we articulated all the elements of this process clearly to everyone involved, or have we made assumptions? Are we upholding this clarity with consistency? Use the matrix to plot your insights and observations. There's no 'right' place at this stage; just gather data on where it sits for now. The power is in noticing and then courageously determining: What is becoming clearer? What would help us move one step closer to confidence? What do we need to do more of and less of to achieve that?

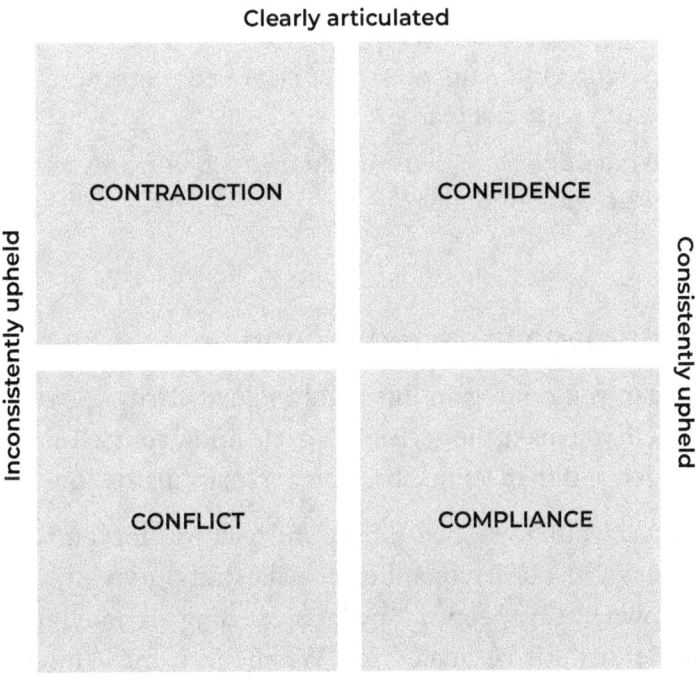

Figure 2.2: The Integrity Matrix

When I work with teams and we use the matrix to review a current practice we follow a process like this. Before we begin I stress to teams to be aware and curious, listen, learn and lean in to what your colleagues are saying and their lived experience. It can be a vulnerable process. It's possible that we'll uncover things we are not pleased about or weren't aware of (those hidden assumptions and habitual ways of acting). I encourage you, just as I encourage my clients, to be aware of the discomfort, notice the urge to blame, and rise above that and return to an attitude of curiosity. Remember, this tool isn't about getting it exactly right. It's about seeing clearly – so you can lead more intentionally.

JOURNAL PROMPTS

- Where in my leadership am I acting from clarity and consistency?
- Where might I be showing up from compliance – doing the thing, but unsure why?
- Where is there unspoken conflict or contradiction that needs light, not blame?
- What's one small shift I could make to bring myself closer to confidence?

The pilgrimage to sacred ground

So what can you do to gain this highly valued clarity you're reading about? Well, you make the decision to get to know yourself as a human and a leader, and then you embark on a transformative journey.

When I was young, we had a beautiful picture storybook version of *Gulliver's Travels*. I remember one illustration vividly: Gulliver pinned down by tiny people, ropes crisscrossing his body, anchoring him to the earth. It fascinated me. Was he in pain? Why didn't he just shake them off and stand up? Surely he was strong enough; he was a giant in that land, after all.

Like Gulliver, we often find ourselves pinned down – not by ropes, but by expectations, obligations or the stories we tell ourselves. The journey to sacred ground is both an evolution and a pilgrimage where we discover and loosen those constraints.

A pilgrimage is not a short journey, nor is it an easy one. It requires patience, resilience and openness to discomfort. Drawing on Phil Cousineau's definition, Parker Palmer describes a pilgrimage as 'a transformative journey to a sacred centre' – one in which the hardships aren't accidental but integral. Treacherous terrain, getting lost, taking a fall – all of it is part of the process, stripping away illusion and making space for the true self to emerge.

Your pilgrimage to sacred ground will offer you opportunities to revisit familiar territory and discover new lands. Approach this pilgrimage with curiosity rather than judgement. Bring a willingness to zoom in and examine the details and, at times, to zoom out and see the whole picture. Over time, the connections between what you do, why you do it and who you are will become clearer. And that clarity? It's what will allow you to shake off what has held you down and stand up, push the hair off your face and step forward so that people can see and hear you.

Start somewhere

I once spotted the phrase 'Start Somewhere' on a coffee mug and, for some reason – possibly because I can be a world-class procrastinator – I've carried it with me ever since (the slogan, not the mug!). The first step in this journey of creating, mapping and getting to know your sacred ground is to start somewhere. Start by committing to being the best human and leader you can be. Get curious about what that might look like. Dream, vision and imagine it.

Grounded leaders start where their feet are – and that's where I invite you to begin this next evolution of your transformative journey. Start right where you are right now. Pause. Reflect. Ask yourself, 'Where am I at right now? Am I happy with that? What would I like to focus on, grow or improve?'

We have the Grounded Leadership Framework to guide our journey, and we'll begin delving into that in the next chapter.

We don't want to over-engineer this journey, though. Think about some of the great adventures you've been on. Did you plan every step of the way, or did you just have an idea of where you wanted to end up and some loose plans on how to get there? When I travel, I like to have a sense of where I'm going and have a few places I'm curious about on my 'must see' list, but I leave plenty of space for discovery and spontaneity. My friend Maria, whom I've been lucky to travel with more than once, likes spontaneity, too, but only once she's mapped out – on a spreadsheet – where she's going, how she'll get there, and where she'll stay when she arrives. You might locate your preference somewhere else on the spectrum. My point is, if we spend too long at the outset of the journey planning, preparing and crafting outcomes, we risk getting stuck in the detail and perhaps even allowing our fear to hold us up, to keep us in the busywork of preparation instead of taking the courageous leap to see what we can discover.

As humans we like to jump to action and to solve problems. As educators, planning actions and next steps is what we do. Jumping straight to action is a leap directly onto the linear path and it means we miss the opportunities and possibilities that the curved path offers us. In his poem of the same name, David Whyte encourages us to resist the urge to immediate action and instead, 'Start close in'. When I'm starting to coach someone, after we've established a goal or a desired outcome, we create a roadmap that plots out the milestones on the client's journey. I've noticed during this process that most clients jump straight to 'doing': identifying the action they think they'll take. That's where I always intervene. I believe it's the purpose of coaching – and the value it adds – to help a client consider ideas or concepts they haven't before and to help them explore things in a different way.

Action should be the second or third step. If we jump straight to action, we simply do things the way we've always done them. We rely on what we already know. For this journey to be transformative, we need to start close in.

In the journey to grounded leadership, starting close in means making the decision to lead, knowing fully that there will be discomfort, vulnerability and the experience of confusion, of not knowing or being sure. My colleague Tracey Ezard shared the following words from Nassim Nicholas Taleb with her LinkedIn community:

> *The most interesting thing about evolution is that it only works because of its antifragility. It is in love with stressors, randomness, uncertainty and disorder.* (Taleb, 2012)

'Stressors, randomness, uncertainty and disorder' sounds a lot like chaos to me. And as school leaders (and readers of the preceding chapters of this book), not only are we ready for chaos, we know it's a prerequisite for clarity.

When we're unsure, when we don't want to take the next step, ensuring we have clarity of purpose, including tapping into a purpose bigger than ourselves, can be a helpful anchor and motivator. Whyte echoed this when he discussed his poem with interviewer Tami Simon. He said, 'You're learning how to find your own place, but you're not doing it ... so you can become the greatest "me" in the world. You're doing it in order to find the ground of your own attentiveness to the rest of the world' (Whyte, 2010).

My invitation to you now, as you prepare to take this transformative journey, is to name your purpose. Clarify why you're committed to taking this journey to sacred ground, and to grounded leadership.

JOURNAL PROMPTS

- What is coming up for you around the concept of 'chaos'?
- Complete this sentence: 'I'm committing to this pilgrimage of mapping my sacred ground so that…'
- What might 'start close in' mean to you?
- Have you made the decision to lead in a grounded way?
- What might your first step – the step before leaping into grand action – be?

Mapping your sacred ground

Essential to every great adventure story is a memorable map. I remember creating a treasure map for a school project in Year 6, tearing the edges and staining the project paper with cold tea to give it the authentic olde-worlde look – as if it were a map some explorer or pirate had lost, leaving them bereft of the treasure I had so creatively placed under a big red 'X' at the centre of the map.

When I was in Ireland in 2024 I had the opportunity to go for long walks through the forest and visit ancient sites. Sometimes the directions were scarce, or in what I've experienced as the Irish fashion: hilariously contradictory. Sometimes as I searched for the trailhead I would be a bit nervous, a bit unsure. I could look at the trail map on the page or on my screen, but a map is not the land, and translating the trail map to my surroundings was at times difficult. I noticed that each time I found the trailhead and began the hike, I would feel a sense of relief and surety. Even though I was usually the only one hiking, it gave me some comfort, some sense of security, to know that the path had been mapped and that others had been there before me. With that sense of certainty I was able to let go of some of my hesitation and allow myself to focus on the hike, enjoy the surroundings and allow my mind to wander, creating the conditions for new thoughts and inspirations to present themselves.

Leader, that's what I have in mind as I write this book. My wish is that, as you commence the journey of mapping your sacred ground, I might be able to help you by offering a map. Perhaps this book might be your trailhead. Of course, as I said, a map is not the landscape – it's a representation of it, and it's not until you start hiking that the actual landscape will reveal itself to you. Your journey, your map and your sacred ground will be unique to you, and that is how it should be. But know that others, including myself, have travelled the path before you.

We all want certainty – to know where to go and exactly which path to follow. But leadership doesn't work like that; there is no 'X marks the spot'. The work itself forms the reward; the discoveries you will make about yourself are the treasures. These discoveries may take the form of insights you gain, patterns you see, strengths you come to recognise and reactions you come to understand more deeply or broadly. These are your treasures. The ability to successfully navigate once-feared situations or interactions is a rich treasure just waiting for you. And unlike a single X on a map, these treasures will keep appearing as long as you keep exploring.

Maps are tools for making sense of the world, but they only make sense if we maintain them. Modern maps are dynamic – they evolve as new information becomes available. Just think about the features available via a GPS mapping service such as Google Maps – you can see real-time traffic congestion, speed cameras, stalled vehicles and obstacles on the road. And as users of these services we can interact with them and feed them information to keep them up-to-date. Our input adds value and relevance to our own map as well as the maps for other users.

Maps are helpful tools for giving us the lay of the land and helping us make sense of our surroundings, but we must be careful not to cling to them as certainty. We must be open to updating and reconfiguring our maps as our understanding shifts. Dynamism and flexibility are important aptitudes to embody as a leader, particularly when it comes to our maps of how we see and understand the world. At the very least, grounded leaders remain aware that when change happens we can be tempted to cling to our old and familiar maps, trying to fit the change into them, rather than being open to considering a new or different interpretation.

The notion of discovery through challenge isn't new; pilgrims, seekers and adventurers have always faced hardship in pursuit of something greater. Cheryl Strayed captures this so well in her memoir *Wild* (Strayed, 2012), the story of her transformative journey as she hiked 1770 kilometres along the Pacific Crest Trail in North America. It was in reading *Wild* that I encountered Adrienne Rich's poem 'Power' (Rich, 1978), lines from which I have, with apologies to Rich, paraphrased in my mind as, 'The source of your pain is the source of your strength.'

And so it is with sacred ground. Your journey will offer you opportunities to lean into your pain: the moments of fear of not being or knowing enough, of embarrassment or shame. It's in working through these moments and experiences that strength and insight (treasure) can be found.

Pilgrimage is about moving through uncertainty towards whatever the traveller seeks. And just as every traveller relies on a map, we rely on our own metaphorical and mental maps to make sense of leadership and life. But to stay relevant, mental maps, like understanding, must evolve.

Sacred ground isn't static, it's evolving. Committing to curiously exploring allows you to become familiar with your sacred ground, getting clear on the parts that make up who you are and how you lead.

The best leaders don't just follow maps – they interact with them, question them and contextualise them, seeking clarity for themselves and others. They recognise when the landscape has changed and have the courage to sit with the discomfort of chaos rather than cling to an outdated map.

JOURNAL PROMPTS

- Do you have any maps that are feeling outdated or no longer serving you like they once did?
- What comes up for you when you consider that the source of your pain is the source of your strength?
- What might 'curiously exploring' require of you as you do this work of mapping sacred ground?

CHAPTER THREE

THE GROUNDED LEADERSHIP FRAMEWORK

Authentic leaders begin with the will and commitment within to work on themselves.

Professor Nancy Koehn

In yoga, we spend time and focus on getting anchored. Depending on the pose, we might be engaging our feet, our hands, our core muscles or a combination. Without being intentional and aware of our anchors we risk forcing ourselves into a shape, making it harder than it needs to be. In this state we can't do as much, reach as far, execute as well. And we can't then relax into the pose and breathe, because we are focused on holding it all together, trying to stay in that forced shape.

The same is true in leadership. Without anchoring ourselves – getting clear on what matters, what supports us – we risk forcing our way through, perhaps trying to be someone we are not or the leader we think we should be, and then working hard to try to hold it all together. That's where this framework comes in.

My Grounded Leadership Framework can serve as a helpful guide for you as you embark on this journey of mapping your own leadership sacred ground.

Sacred ground is at the heart of this framework. Sacred ground and the four quadrants of this model (shown in figure 3.1) are inextricably woven together and attention to each of the quadrants reinforces, maps and strengthens your sacred ground and in turn, how you show up and lead.

Figure 3.1: The Grounded Leadership Framework

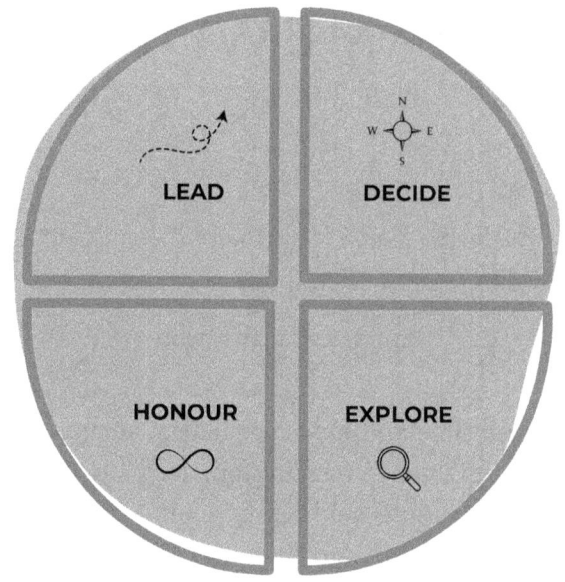

The framework itself has been through its own evolution. It began as a series of scribbled circles on my office whiteboard, each one a stepping stone that I observed leaders take on their journey – defining, refining and ultimately stepping into the leader they aspired to be. I realised that I too had taken many of those same steps in my journey to becoming the leader and human I am.

As more and more leaders shared their stories with me, the scribbles became more defined. The edges firmed up as I began to see with greater clarity and definition each 'stage' of the framework.

Not only did each stage become clearer, but so too did the map of the journey. Those circles were not discrete stepping stones – they were more interconnected than that. And the road wasn't linear – it was circular, ever-evolving. So for now, the Grounded Leadership Framework looks as it does; but I expect it will continue to evolve and expand as I learn, experiment and reflect on it and how leaders embody and apply it.

Neither the work of leadership, nor the growth and evolution of leaders, is solitary work. While solitude plays a crucial role, so too do connection, reflection, feedback and community.

Let's take a brief trip around the framework, beginning with *Decide* and moving in a clockwise direction.

Decide on the leader you aspire to be

The Decide quadrant of the framework is a crucial, foundational layer in your sacred ground. It calls you to clarify where you're going, who you want to be as a leader, and the difference you want to make in the world (vision), as well as your internal anchor and compass (values).

Explore the human you are

Explore adds the depth, the light and the shadow, the ballast and the shape to your sacred ground as you explore the human you are with your strengths, challenges, habits, shadows and stories.

Honour the practices that help you show up

Honour adds flexibility and strength to your leadership and anchors you more deeply through regular devotion to the practices that sustain and nurture you.

Lead the way and make things happen

Lead takes all of this focus and dedication and ensures that your sacred ground does not become an elaborate construction for your own enjoyment, but rather that your work is in service of others, skilfully guiding, communicating and supporting them to navigate their own path.

You'll notice in the framework that all four quadrants are of equal size. That's because no one quadrant is more important. In this framework attention to each quadrant is what provides the ongoing ballast, the rigour and effectiveness of your sacred ground.

Like a fine wine or an excellent chocolate cake, this framework has layers. It's complex! For one thing, each of the quadrants has a relationship with its diagonally opposite quadrant. Let's take a look at these.

Decide and Honour

Decide is about defining your leadership; Honour is about sustaining it (see figure 3.2).

In Decide we are concerned with getting clear on the leader we want to be, how we want to show up and the values that will guide and anchor us. These are enormously important decisions to make and be clear about, but almost useless if we don't action them. Leaders may have a clear vision of how they want to show up and the difference they want to make, but without Honour, those visions remain just a wish. Honour ensures that your leadership vision remains front and centre and can weather the relentless demands of the role.

The Honour quadrant is largely concerned with your wellbeing and capacity to sustain yourself. The work in this space challenges you to identify – and action, of course – tools and practices that keep you well and protect your energy. By honouring these tools and practices, you create the conditions you require in order to actually *be* the leader you decided you wanted to be in the Decide quadrant of this framework.

Figure 3.2: The Grounded Leadership Framework: Decide and Honour

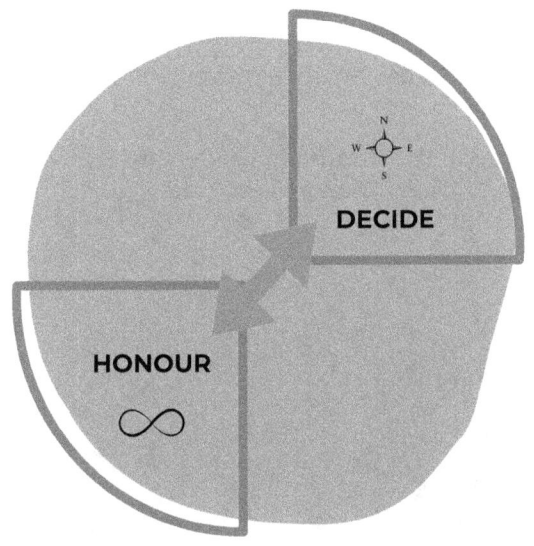

Explore and Lead

Explore is about looking inward; Lead is about how you step forward (see figure 3.3).

In Explore you'll be doing the vital work of deepening self-awareness. You'll be examining your strengths, your habits and your stories – all the stuff that can help or hinder you (although often they do both). Armed with this understanding of who you are and why you do what you do, you'll be well positioned to understand how your behaviours and actions impact others. You'll deepen your empathy, and your ability to recognise that in any situation, others are experiencing their own internal realities. You'll see beyond actions to the emotions and stories that may be driving them, fostering true human-to-human connection.

Lead focuses largely on communication: how we interact and share meaning and messages. This includes the easy conversations and those that are not so fun – such as critical feedback or courageous conversations that not many of us look forward to having, let alone having to initiate. But, grounded in the self-awareness, empathy and emotional intelligence you focused on developing in Explore, you are well positioned to have truly human-centred conversations.

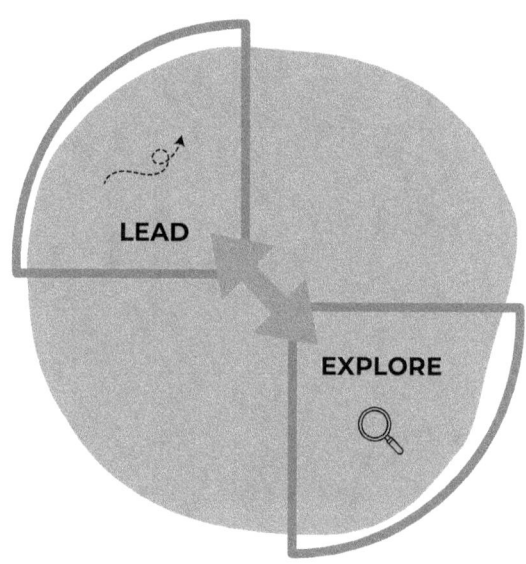

Figure 3.3: The Grounded Leadership Framework: Explore and Lead

Grounded leaders aren't just clear and purposeful communicators, they are self-aware and attuned to the people they are in communication with. Explore helps you build that awareness, and Lead helps you apply it practically.

Internal and external work

As my work with the Grounded Leadership Framework continues and my understanding has deepened, I've come to think of the right side of the framework (Decide and Explore) as the 'internal work': the work we do on, to and with ourselves. This includes identifying our values, deciding on the leader we want to be and how we want to make a difference. The left side of the framework (Honour and Lead) is more about external work. It's outward-facing and, in many cases, visible to others – the wellbeing practices, the boundaries, the conversations, the language we use with our colleagues and teams.

The Grounded Leadership Framework invites you to deep reflection and calls you to action. Doing the work of each quadrant 'awakens you to the integrity of your inner power' (O'Donohue, 1997) which is affirming and empowering and exciting. But this journey, this framework, will also awaken you to the moments when you are not in integrity with that power. In my experience, these moments feel less like an awakening and more like watching a scary movie with your hands clasped over your face, peering between your fingers just enough to soften the blow.

Figure 3.4: The Grounded Leadership Framework: internal and external work

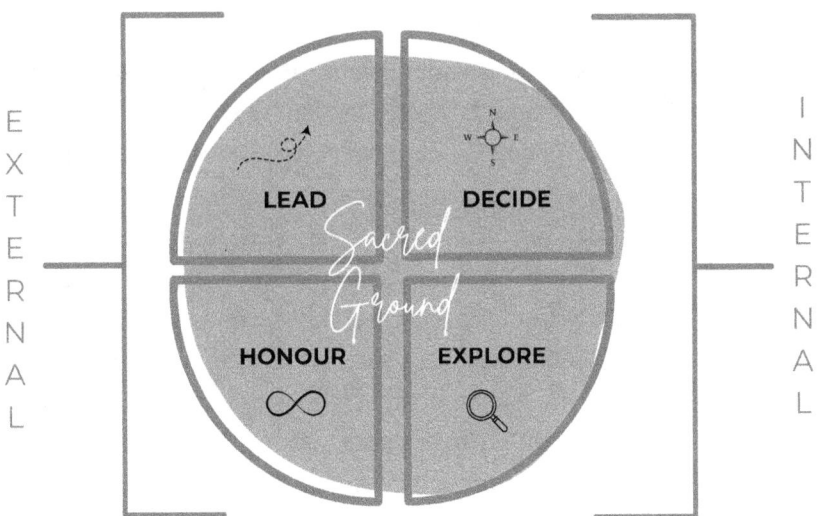

Remember, this is not a one-and-done framework; rather it is a continuing evolution. Think of an upwards spiral – rising and expanding as it evolves. As you evolve, revisiting each of the stages of the framework again and again, you'll add depth and nuance to your sacred ground – to that which holds you steady, allows you to bounce back and gives you the courage to be your authentic self.

> **JOURNAL PROMPTS**
> - What's coming up for you in this early introduction to the framework?
> - Are there parts you're looking forward to visiting?
> - Is there a particular quadrant you're already feeling aversion to?
>
> There's no right or wrong answer here, but exploring your thoughts and feelings at this early stage may offer you some interesting insights.

A note about the internal work

It's tempting to believe that leadership is all about strategies, meetings, timetables, emails and data. As a leader, it's easy to be consumed by these things every day. This means that the kind of internal work required to map your sacred ground can feel indulgent, like something you just don't have time for. But in my experience, leaders who haven't paused to do this work often end up leading on autopilot. They're the ones who are pulled in every direction by the loudest voice or the next crisis. In a world where burnout is high and complexity is the norm, it's the leaders who are clear on their values, who are grounded in something deeper than 'doing', who create the calm in the storm. When you're grounded in who you are and what matters most, your decisions become clearer, your presence steadier. That's the kind of leadership we need now more than ever.

The good news is that the foundations of your sacred ground are already there. The map is already outlined; you've probably stood upon your ground for balance and direction at least once in your life so far. At the very least, you have values – even if you can't name them yet, they have been developing since you were an infant. It's thought that values are set in place between the ages of 10 and 20.

Think of a time when you stood up for what you believed in. It may have been uncomfortable, but you found you just could not suppress what you believed in. What exactly happened? What were you feeling? As you explore the memory you may discover that one or more of your non-negotiables was at the heart of your stand.

Lonnie, a deputy principal I worked with, spent years leading without having done the internal work I write about. She knew what she liked and disliked but she hadn't ever articulated the deep, guiding principles that influenced her choices. That changed during our work together. Lonnie intentionally defined her core values and discovered that they – kindness, integrity and trust – had been with her all along. In the creative, sense-making style I've come to know and admire Lonnie for, she named her values her KIT Bag (see what she did there?).

This wasn't just a creative metaphor for Lonnie – she lived it. Just as she always carried a physical kit bag for work, hobbies or emergencies, her values were always with her, shaping her leadership.

But her kit bag wasn't just about practical problem-solving. It was also her moral compass. When a particular situation at work challenged her integrity, she couldn't let it go – not because of any practical implications, but because it struck at her very core.

A fellow leader had made a decision that, while seemingly small, undermined a shared understanding within the leadership team. Others on the team dismissed it as 'just one of those things'. But to Lonnie it wasn't just a one-off issue – it was the opposite of what she believed leadership should be.

She wrestled with the situation and her reaction to it, questioning whether she was overreacting. But the more she thought about it, the more she realised that this wasn't just about a single decision – it was about how she showed up as a leader and the impact that had on the school culture. If she let this go, she would be signalling that she accepted the situation and she'd be compromising on what she valued most highly.

So, she took action – despite the discomfort of calling out one of her colleagues and team members. She directly and respectfully shared with the team member what she was conflicted about and why it mattered. It was a necessary discussion, but it wasn't easy. However, in bravely initiating that conversation, Lonnie signalled to her team that integrity and trust were not just values that she espoused in words, they were the foundation she stood on.

> **JOURNAL PROMPTS**
>
> You may not have a Lonnie-like story, but I promise you, you have a kit bag!
>
> - When have you strongly stood on your sacred ground, having a feeling of not being able to stay quiet about something?
> - What did it cost you?
> - What did it bring you?

The Grounded Leadership Check-In

The Grounded Leadership Check-In is designed to help you reflect on your current reality as a leader. It's a simple self-assessment, aligned to the Grounded Leadership Framework we are exploring in this book. It will give insights into your strengths and areas for growth: keep them in mind as we explore the framework in greater depth. Rather than a deeply diagnostic assessment, this check-in is designed to help you tune in as you embark on this journey. To get real value from this check-in, notice the internal chatter that comes up as you take the quiz. That's where the real insights often lie!

Instructions

For each statement, rate yourself from 1 to 5, where:

1 = I'm just beginning to develop this area
2 = I do this occasionally
3 = I'm building consistency
4 = I do this often and with intention
5 = This is a core strength of mine

Write down your scores, then total them at the end.

Decide – Leading with clarity and intentionality

1. When making decisions, I rely on my core values and vision to guide me.
2. I am clear about my leadership vision and can communicate it effectively.
3. I am willing to push the hair off my face and speak out.

Explore – Cultivating self-awareness and growth

4. I regularly take time to reflect on my leadership growth and areas for improvement.
5. I recognise and manage my emotions effectively to maintain a positive leadership presence.
6. I am aware of my internal chatter and the stories I regularly tell myself.

Honour – Nurturing wellbeing and connection

7. I create space to switch off from work, allowing myself time to recharge and refocus.
8. I am able to prioritise my own wellbeing.
9. I practise self-compassion, acknowledging my efforts and progress without self-judgement.

Lead – Empowering and supporting others

10. I foster a collaborative environment where team members feel encouraged to share ideas and contribute to the team's goals.
11. I communicate clearly and confidently, ensuring my team understands expectations and feels empowered to take ownership of tasks.
12. I approach courageous conversations with openness and respect, addressing challenges clearly.

Scoring and results

Total your score and match it to the descriptions below:

- **48–60 → Grounded and confident leader**
  You have strong clarity in your leadership, balancing decision-making, self-reflection, and connection. You are leading with alignment and strength. Keep building on these foundations!

- **36–47 → Intentional leader**
  You are developing solid leadership habits and creating real impact. Strengthening one or two key areas will allow you to lead with even more ease and confidence.

- **24–35 → Evolving leader**
  You are actively growing and refining your leadership. Recognising your strengths and making intentional shifts will help you step further into your leadership potential.

- **12–23 → Emerging leader**
  You are in the early stages of defining your leadership approach. Small, steady steps in clarity, confidence and connection will help you gain momentum. Leadership is an evolving journey – one step at a time.

I'm inviting you now to make a decision. Are you willing to conduct an experiment with me, to see if perhaps you are exactly smart enough, experienced enough, confident enough, old enough and wise enough to step up and lead with grounded confidence?

It's not the only decision you'll have to make of course – leadership can be a deluge of decisions. Some you'll get right, others you'll wish you'd done differently – that's to be expected.

This decision, right now, to test the hypothesis that you have the makings of an extraordinary, authentic leader, is both exciting and vomit-inducing. It's terrifying and at the same time filled with hope and possibility.

Are you in?

CHAPTER FOUR

DECIDE

Decide on the leader you aspire to be

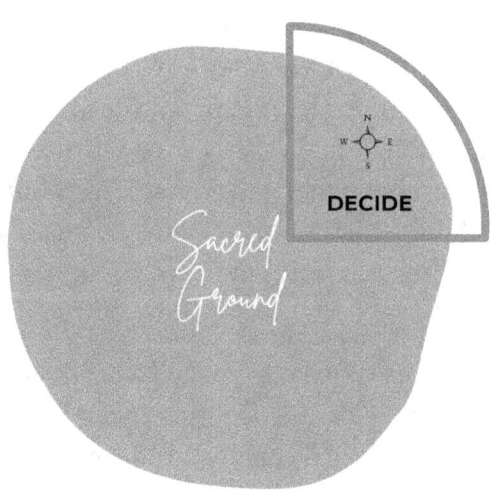

One of my mentors, Matt, says that leadership is a decision, not a position. As a school leader you know that a typical day involves myriad decisions – some days so many that we can feel like we are spinning. The Decide phase of the Grounded Leadership Framework is about pausing long enough to tune into some of our beliefs and values – those things that shape how we show up and that inform the decisions we make.

In this chapter, we'll explore what it means to choose with purpose – especially when the path ahead isn't neatly mapped. We'll reflect on the values and vision that sit at the heart of our leadership, and consider what becomes possible when we choose to lead from that place.

Our work here is not about having all the answers, it's about getting curious and then clear about what matters, and then letting that clarity shape how we lead.

On the first day of the Emerging and Middle Leaders Project (a transformative 12-month professional learning journey for school leaders, guided by the Grounded Leadership Framework), we begin by sharing some of the experiences and challenges we've encountered so far in our leadership journey. Some of the participants are brand new to leadership, while others have been in their role for many years. I'm no longer surprised when most participants, no matter how much time they've served, share that they didn't actually put themselves forward for leadership – instead they'd been 'tapped on the shoulder'. Many say they 'never saw themselves as a leader'. *They* might not have seen themselves as a leader, but someone had, and now they found themselves about to embark on a personal and professional learning journey, perhaps unlike any they have done before.

What *did* surprise me was what happened when I relayed this insight to a room full of principals and deputy principals. In response there was a resounding acknowledgement and affirmation of the emerging leader experience. These seasoned leaders recalled feeling exactly the same way as the new and middle leaders when they began their journey. What's more, they still felt it from time to time. By now they had made the decision to be a leader, to lead their community and embrace the discomfort of not feeling enough. But at their heart, they were humans, with human brains wired for safety and connection – brains that, whether they realise it or not, are constantly scanning and assessing to ensure they are in a safe and connected state.

This constant internal comparison and concern for 'fitting in' can make us hold back our genuine thoughts, emotions and reactions. We fear that we'll be discovered as the imposter our inner critic tells us we are: not experienced enough, not qualified enough, not fun enough, not *enough*. Instead of risking the judgement and shame of being 'found out', we adopt the role we think we 'should' portray, trying to be how a leader who is perfectly 'enough' should be.

In a room full of humans being what they think they 'should' be, imagine the impact when someone is brave enough to share what's really going on for them. It's liberating, and it opens the door to deeper conversation, genuine connection and empathy.

Clara, a principal I worked with in a community of practice, captured this power so beautifully. After guiding the participants to have a coaching conversation with another principal, I asked the group to share their insights. Clara took a breath, looked around the room, and said, 'You know what? It's just good to know I'm not the only one running a shitshow!' The room erupted in laughter – not just because it was funny, but because it was true. There was relief in the honesty, in the shared recognition that leadership can feel like barely holding it together some days. But in that moment, something shifted. The weight of isolation lifted. The conversation that followed wasn't about leaders demonstrating all the great things they were doing, papering over the cracks and rough spots. Instead, they ripped the paper off and got real. There was great value and connection forged in that session where they clearly and honestly discovered they weren't alone in the chaos and that maybe, just maybe, they were doing better than they thought.

At the outset of my work with emerging and middle leaders, many of them are yet to make the decision to step fully into leadership. They have been awarded the title; hopefully they've been allocated time to execute the extra responsibilities their role brings; and fingers crossed they've received at least a small pay increase and maybe even some dedicated office space! Because of those visible signals and symbols of leadership, their colleagues are expecting them to *be* a leader. I laugh as I remember one of the emerging and middle leaders recounting their experience with this: 'It's as if my colleagues think I magically came to know everything overnight.'

The bottom line is, these leaders are already being called to make decisions, and daily.

It's generally about midway through the 12-month Emerging and Middle Leaders Project that participants begin to bravely voice their commitment and decision to lead. As one participant so beautifully articulated a belief that they'd been nurturing throughout the project: 'I *do* have something important to offer and I'm ready to share it and try and make a difference.'

It's no coincidence to me that participants generally experience this shift about halfway through the project. That timing coincides with us being about halfway through the Grounded Leadership Framework quadrants. Participants have had time to craft a vision; they've defined their values and done a whole lot of exploring of their stories, strengths, challenges and habits. The first half of the framework is largely internal work, and that's what these participants have immersed themselves in, so that by the midpoint they emerge courageously ready to take their seat at the leadership table – sitting, as my mentor-from-afar Jerry Colonna wrote, 'as if they've a right to be there' (Colonna, 2019).

Claim the Day

Many times a day, we get to decide how we want to show up and what type of leader we want to be – not just overall, but in each situation and interaction. When I began coaching leaders and facilitating workshops for educators, one of the first practices I created was 'Claim the Day'. I encouraged leaders to Claim the Day before they even got out of bed in the morning, before they began mentally rehearsing and shuffling their to-do lists.

Back then, only ten years ago, mobile phones weren't the all-consuming arm-extensions they have become, so I didn't need to remind them to do this exercise before they picked up their phone – but for most of us modern-day, perpetually electronically connected beings, we need the reminder.

> **GROUNDED LEADERSHIP PRACTICE**
>
> Each morning, before you get going and get busy, decide how *you* will show up. Before you get out of bed, before your feet hit the floor, claim the day as yours. Name a word that describes how you want to be today, and get out there and be it!
>
> Importantly, pause throughout the day and check in on how you are doing. For example, if you claimed that today you would be 'patient', check in on how you're doing with that. Doing well? Great, keep going! Forgotten all about it? Reset and start over.
>
> Remember, you can't do much about others' moods and behaviours, but you are 100 per cent able to choose how you will show up.

Recently I've made an addition to Claim the Day – a prequel, if you will. It comes from Jerry Lynch who, among his prolific authoring, wrote about 'winning the day' (Lynch, 2024). I've adopted his practice of taking five slow, deep breaths before getting up in the morning. I do this when I wake and then I shift my awareness to the day ahead and feel ready to intentionally Claim the Day.

The idea of 'claiming' brings to mind explorers who literally stake their claim, intentionally and definitively. And surely that's how we want to start our day as leaders: with clarity of intention and direction. After all, this decision is not insignificant. In fact, as

Margaret Wheatley declares, 'I can't imagine a more important task than to consciously choose who I want to be as a leader for this time' (Wheatley, 2023).

Claiming the day is one thing – what actually comes at you when you step into the school building is quite another! How we deal with whatever comes at us is of course another series of decisions we make based on the situation and our experience, values, wisdom, emotional intelligence and state at the time.

Engaging in the work of the Grounded Leadership Framework is the result of a decision, and each stage of the framework invites further and multiple decisions.

Reflection is essential. This can be uncomfortable, particularly when we are sitting in the vulnerability and discomfort of reflecting on the decisions we've made or not made and why, and the implications of those decisions.

This is where leadership truly begins. The Decide stage is about defining your vision of the leader you aspire to be and the impact you aspire to have. It's about defining and anchoring yourself in the values that will guide you forward. Because leadership is a decision to lead, and to lead with intention.

JOURNAL PROMPTS

- Are you prepared to commit time and energy to doing this work, both the practical actions and the dedicated reflection?
- What will this look like in practical terms?
- What might get in your way?
- How will you stay committed to your practice?

Decide: A vision that draws you forward

Can you remember your first leadership role in a school? Maybe you took on the role of a middle leader, assistant leader or coordinator of a curriculum area or project. Perhaps you applied and went through an interview process, or maybe you were tapped on the shoulder. Whatever your circumstance, I'm sure you had at least a few hopes, dreams or intentions around the impact you might make, the changes you could help bring about, and how you could make that particular area of your stewardship *better*.

Did you have a clear and compelling vision of the leader you wanted to be and the goals for the school or team you were leading? It's perfectly okay to admit if you didn't. In fact, recently a school principal whom I worked with when I was a teacher and whom, to this day, I consider to be one of the most exceptional leaders I've come across, challenged me on the idea of leadership vision. 'I didn't have a clear vision when I started this work of leadership,' he said. 'I just thought I could contribute something and this school might benefit from it.' I could argue here that he *did* have a vision, albeit an unformed one, but that's not the point. The point I'm trying to make is that a perfectly polished vision is not the goal, nor is a compelling vision a requirement to beginning your leadership journey.

However, as you take your seat as a leader, deciding how you want to show up, knowing how you want to lead and being clear on the impact you want to have is most definitely necessary. After all, as the Cheshire Cat famously said, if you don't know where you're going, anywhere will do…

Leaders need a vision that they genuinely believe in and feel motivated to get up each morning to bring to life. To echo the sentiment of my former principal, though: *you don't have to have one to get started*. In fact, you don't have to have one of your own at all, according to Simon Sinek – just find someone else's that you can get behind, adopt it, and get on with it (Sinek, 2025)!

Crafting a vision, creating a vision board, choosing just the right words and metaphors, images and colours – these activities can be useful and motivating, clarifying even. But beware: they can also be pathways of procrastination to get lost down.

Anyone who has worked in a school for more than a year or two will probably have been involved in the creation of a school vision statement. In my own experience, it wasn't always a fun time. When I am asked now to help a school or team craft their vision statement, I am guided by this principle: the words don't matter as much as how we actually live out the vision. Business guru Jim Collins said it much more eloquently: 'Great performance is about 1% vision and 99% alignment' (Collins, 2001).

How we spend our days is of course how we spend our lives (Dillard, 1989). In schools, how we spend our days is fast, jam-packed, focused on getting things done, making progress and dealing with whatever unexpected events have come our way.

Unless we courageously slow down and are intentional about how we show up, about what drives us and about how we spend each day, we run the risk that the pace, the administration and the job will drive us, will become our life and will eventually do us in.

How we show up matters. It's too important to leave to chance or until we 'get a chance'. Grounded leaders:

- decide how we want to show up
- are clear about what motivates us and what we are driven to achieve
- regularly make time to check in on how we're doing.

Your vision will adjust and become more nuanced over time. Your job, as you evolve as leader and human, is to allow the space for your vision to evolve as well. Free it from the unforgiving lens of perfectionism and the urgent voice of the inner critic who drives you to *get it done now* so that you can share it and prove to others that you are good enough, well-prepared enough and organised enough to lead.

A few years ago Jack, a school leader, engaged me to be his coach. Jack had lost his joy in the job. In our first conversation, I noticed that his language was cynical and sharp and he seemed truly exhausted. He was quick to blame the system, the role and himself for the way he was feeling. He couldn't see a way out.

'I don't know how much longer I can do this,' he admitted.

My new client was drowning – not because he wasn't capable, but because he didn't have an anchor to ground him or a vision for his leadership that compelled and excited him, providing him with ballast and buoyancy or filling him with the grit he needed when times were tough. Instead, the demands of the role had begun to grind him down and he was in danger of giving up.

Jack is another one of those humans I consider to be an exceptional leader and school principal. He is intelligent and deeply connected to his values. This connection just wasn't clear at the time we started working together. The turning point for Jack came in an unexpected way – via a simple visioning exercise.

One of the early exercises we did together was visualising the future he desired to create. It was an incredibly powerful experience for him. He reported that it allowed him to tap into a past experience at another school – a time when he had felt deeply fulfilled and aligned with his purpose. Staying really present in the visioning exercise, he could feel the pride, excitement and energy of that time as if it were happening all over again.

Over the following days and weeks, Jack felt his passion for the work reignite. His determination returned – not because the challenges had disappeared, but because he had something to work towards again. He was stepping into a future that wasn't yet visible, but now, he believed in it. Hope had replaced cynicism. But Jack knew that vision alone wasn't enough: action was required. And to take that action, he had to fully commit to being the leader he aspired to be and doing the work required to bring about his vision.

It really was amazing to me how that simple visioning exercise transformed Jack's attitude. Being able to tap into a powerful past experience and actually feel the emotions of that time was enough for him to begin to rekindle his passion for the job. Don't get me wrong, it wasn't a miracle moment – Jack still had work to do – but it was a significant milestone and turnaround point.

It can take time, experience and experimentation to develop a clear and compelling vision that feels like a good fit. Your vision may go through many iterations. If you're not sure, start with your core values – these don't change very much over your lifetime – and build from there.

Everyone has to start somewhere. Don't let a lack of the 'perfect vision' make you think you're not ready to lead. Start at the heart: what you value. Grab a bit of inspiration from others, dream big, get inspired and vision something 'audacious' (as Jim Collins would say).

JOURNAL PROMPTS

- What might happen if you took the time to visualise the leader you dream of being and the future you want to create?
- Who is the leader you want to be?
- How do you want to show up for others and serve them?
- What audacious difference do you dream of making?

GROUNDED LEADERSHIP PRACTICE

Leader, there are no rules here. Your vision can be long or short. It can be a poem, a vision board, an image, an essay, an AI-generated image, a sentence. It's your vision; you do you. It's the purpose that matters, as well as the process. Be alert and aware as you craft your vision:

- What do you notice about what's important to you?
- What stories do you notice popping up? (Especially notice any stories of doubt or dismissal, such as 'That'll never work', 'Who do you think you are?' or 'That's way too big – settle down'.)
- Which parts of your vision get you excited and inspired?
- Which parts can you clearly see? Which parts require a little more teasing out?

You can also access a recording of my vision-crafting exercise to guide you through this process at **katrinabourke.com**.

Vision and values as touchstones

In ancient times, a touchstone was a small, smooth slab of dark stone relied on by traders and goldsmiths from civilisations as far back as Mesopotamia, Ancient Greece and Rome to test the purity of precious metals. They would take a piece of supposedly precious metal – perhaps a gold coin being offered in trade – and rub it against the touchstone, leaving behind a mark. By comparing the mark to those made by known pure metals, they could quickly tell whether the gold was genuine or mixed with other metals. It was a simple tool, but essential. It allowed merchants to see past the shiny surface and determine what was beneath.

Alan, a wise teacher of mine – himself a grounded and authentic leader – used the metaphor of touchstones to teach me and other school leaders about values. I remember that learning experience well; I was a new deputy principal, on my very first leadership conference, gathered together with colleagues on retreat in a beautiful venue, surrounded by nature. There was a slowed-down, relaxed pace, good food and drinks, and time to reflect – all the things dreams are made of for busy school leaders!

That was many years ago, but Alan's wisdom has stayed with me. One story he told stood out in particular – his own experience as a first-time principal. Within weeks of stepping into the role, he faced a difficult challenge: a staff member was bullying one colleague and actively undermining another. Alan knew he had to act. He was clear on his message: this behaviour was unacceptable, it had no place in the school, and if it didn't change immediately, the staff member would face disciplinary action and/or have to leave.

As a new principal – and a genuinely compassionate person – Alan felt sick about the conversation ahead. But before stepping into that meeting, he anchored himself in his values and vision for the type of leader he wanted to be, reminding himself that how he handled the moment mattered as much as the decision itself. His values would guide him through.

The conversation was difficult. The staff member didn't take it well. As they exited the room, they firmly shut the door behind them. Alan sat there for a moment, his heart pounding. As he retold the story to us he admitted that when the staff member had gone, he felt like reaching for the rubbish bin and throwing up!

But despite the discomfort, when he reflected on the conversation he reassured himself that he could hold his head high. He had navigated the conversation in a way that honoured his values and vision – both as a leader and as a human.

So often in leadership, we navigate situations where there is not a happy or win-win solution for all involved. It's uncomfortable, not least because our human brain signals 'threat' when we are out of connection or relationship with others. Knowing our values and acting in alignment with them, being anchored in our vision, supports us to withstand the discomfort of such situations. Importantly, it means we do not shy away from difficult but necessary conversations.

In this way, values are non-negotiable. Alan could not have kept quiet about the behaviour of his staff member, knowing what he knew and seeing the impact of their actions on the rest of the community. Aside from his professional responsibilities as a school leader, the staff member's behaviour violated Alan's values.

Shalom H Schwartz is widely recognised as one of the world's leading researchers in human values. He wrote:

> *Values serve as standards or criteria. Values guide the selection or evaluation of actions, policies, people, and events. People decide what is good or bad, justified or illegitimate, worth doing or avoiding, based on possible consequences for their cherished values.* (Schwartz 2012)

Alan also could not have held his head up high at the end of the conversation if he had resorted to anger, blame, deceit or 'soft-selling' his concerns when talking with the staff member. Any of those approaches would have been outside his values. Even though the staff member's behaviour was abhorrent to Alan, being true to his values meant showing them respect and compassion, too.

Values clashes: A hidden source of conflict

We've established by now that our values are our foundation, a vital and solid layer of our sacred ground and, therefore, essential in how we show up and lead. This doesn't make them 'right', though. Our values are so deeply a part of who we are, and have been in place for so long, that by the time we are an adult and leader, it can seem as though they are 'just the way things are'. We often believe that everyone holds these same values as dear and true. It's true that some of our values may be shared by others, particularly in a caring profession such as education. But, of course, not all of our values will completely align with those others hold. Sometimes our values may even clash with those we're working with.

A values clash is not, on its own, a reason for dismissal, but it can be challenging to work with someone we don't see eye-to-eye with on what we consider to be a fundamental and important value.

Schwartz reinforces the often 'hidden' force of values at play, explaining that 'the impact of values in everyday decisions is rarely conscious' (Schwartz, 2012). This is why, when values clash, we rarely recognise it as such. Instead we often label the other person as wrong, rude, unaware, arrogant or even stupid, or fall back on some version of 'them = bad, me = good'. The danger in this is that our assessment of the other becomes the filter through which we interpret all future interactions or scenarios involving that person. This is not a helpful grounding for collaboration and unlikely to help us adopt a posture of curiosity and listening to understand.

And, of course, like so many interpersonal interactions, we often don't realise what actually happened until later. Have you had that experience? You're in a conversation or a meeting and you notice your temperature rising along with your frustration; your buttons are being pushed by another person and very quickly you label them (most likely not out loud!). You might withdraw from the meeting or from contributing to it further. But later, when you've cooled down a little and perhaps received feedback or insight from a critical friend, you can see that the other person wasn't being an annoying nitpicker. Rather, you had a clash of values.

What a grounded, human-centred leader does here is acknowledge the misinterpretation, not just for themselves, but also for the sake of the relationship. They use it as an opportunity to build self-awareness and, where possible, repair the connection.

Staying aligned to your values is staying in integrity with the person you are and that other people know you to be. Staying aligned to your values allows you to reflect and see that you remained in integrity, when sometimes that's the only positive take-away from a situation.

JOURNAL PROMPTS

Pause for a moment and call to mind a colleague you find difficult to work with – someone you feel yourself to be at odds with most of the time.

- What label have you given them?
- Can you set that aside for a few minutes and get curious about what values might be at the heart of their behaviour?
- How is that clashing with your own values?

Values in action

Many years after I met Alan, he helped me navigate my own turbulent time. I was in a workplace that had become quite toxic following some key personnel changes. I had witnessed the leadership team deteriorate firstly to passive-aggressive behaviours and quickly to outright bullying. As a member of that team, my own values of compassion and truth were being crashed into daily as I saw, heard and became the target of the ringleader's openly aggressive behaviour. I raised my concerns on more than one occasion. I addressed the aggressive behaviour, but to no avail: the person involved denied anything had happened and my leader put it back on me to handle, responding to my bid for assistance and connection with a curt, 'What are *you* going to do about it?'

My values of truth and courage were at the heart of me speaking up and naming what was happening in an effort to change the culture of the team and my colleague's behaviour. And it was my value of compassion that kept me in that team for longer than was healthy. I cared for the school community and didn't want to leave them to deal with that behaviour and the fallout of such a drastic change in culture. But in the end all three of my values – truth, courage and compassion – compelled me to leave. I had been true to myself and to my colleagues by trying to change things, but I came to realise that I was suffering. I was not being very kind or compassionate to myself and I was not getting kindness, truth, courage or compassion from the senior leaders I wanted it from.

With Alan's help, my values of truth and compassion became the guiding lights that helped me to leave that place with my head held high. In staying aligned to truth I couldn't stay and pretend it was okay. In staying aligned to truth I had tried to change things. In compassion to myself I had to get out of there. In staying aligned to compassion to my fellow leaders I would not publicly denounce them. It was hard; I wanted to blame and shame them, let others see what was actually going on. I wanted to hurt them the way they had hurt me. The waves were seriously crashing around me in that situation and I was knocked flat on more than one occasion, but with the help of trusted colleagues and friends – and coming back to my values, even clinging to them at times – I was able to navigate that turbulent time. Now, looking back, I'm so very thankful that I can reflect with pride on the situation and see the gift it provided me in knowing the strength and wisdom that values can offer us.

Team values

A couple of years ago, the leadership team at a primary school in Melbourne spent a day with me to define their team vision and values. The conversation I witnessed was extraordinary. I had challenged them to land on just three values that would be non-negotiable and at the heart of how their team operated and made decisions for the school. I had the privilege of sitting back and listening to them explore, suggest, challenge, debate and clarify their way through a list of about 12 values, down to the final three. By the end of that dialogue, they had three values that everyone on the team owned and shared a common definition of. And, more than that, they were deeply committed to those values.

Applying the philosophy that *action is what makes the difference*, they then went on to activate their values, co-creating a document that showed what those values looked like in action for the team, and what it would look like when they were out of alignment.

The conversations this team had took time – a whole day offsite – but the impact is still felt in that team today. Their values and vision are clearly and proudly on the wall of their leadership space, and the definitions and actions are documented there, too. They live it. And when they don't, they feel it and notice it and call each other out on it. It's powerful for them, and for the school community who, on the whole, experience a clear, confident, consistent and curious team of leaders.

Living by your values

I don't believe you necessarily need to profess your values out loud, in public. I do believe you need to live by them. And if you do, people will come to know what they are.

Millie is one of the best leaders I've had the privilege to work with and learn from over many years. I don't think we've ever had a conversation where she has specifically named her values, but I know what at least some of them are. I know she values people, because that is what her actions consistently demonstrate. People are drawn to her, and her staff trust her with their human vulnerabilities. Every morning Millie visits her staff in their offices and classrooms and greets them, following up on family or life events she knows they've been experiencing. After that she stands in the playground, greeting parents and students as they arrive, treating them with the same care and respect. Imagine the impact of those actions: here is a school leader in a notoriously time-poor role, making time for her community. This sends a signal to all in her orbit that they matter to her, that she sees them and values them. But what makes it work, what makes it build trust and relationships and love and loyalty in the team, is that it is genuine. Millie genuinely cares about and values people. If she didn't, if she was pretending to, if she did it out of obligation or because she 'should', it wouldn't ring true. It wouldn't have resonance and people would be on to that from a mile away.

What gives your values power and impact is that you honour them, and you live and act in alignment with them. That's what others notice.

Your values show through in how you show up. Equally, if you profess values because you think you should, or you believe they sound more convenient or desirable than your true values, it will show through.

It's also important to avoid weaponising your values. 'I couldn't help it, I was being true to my values' is not a legitimate excuse for poor behaviour. Ultimately, you choose how you show up and what you say. Just because 'kindness', for example, is not a highly held value for you, it doesn't mean you get to act without it.

The risk of 'fake' values

A member of our first Middle and Emerging Leaders Project, Xavier, gained first-hand experience of the impact and importance of a leader's values. Each time our group met Xavier would share how the experience was unfolding.

Xavier is an avid footy player, and during the year of our project, he had been appointed as co-captain of his footy team. The team members, including Xavier, were excited to welcome a new coach, Liam, and their excitement was only strengthened during their first meeting with him. He outlined his values of teamwork, loyalty and fairness, which gave the team hope and encouragement for the year ahead. His ability to name his values and describe how they would be at the heart of how he showed up and what they could expect from him gave the team confidence.

As the season continued, though, things took a dark turn. Liam's actions, including the way he spoke to certain individuals, began to unnerve the team. What he was doing and saying was not aligned with the values he had professed would be his leadership bedrock. The team was alarmed, and the focus of the leadership team shifted from supporting their coach to one of damage control. While this was happening, Xavier was learning in our Emerging and Middle Leaders group about the importance of alignment with vision and values, the power of knowing one's sacred ground and the difference that can be made by leading with a care for things such as relationships, humility, transparency and high achievement. For Xavier and his team, it was a car wreck of a season, one that Liam didn't even see through until the end: he left prematurely to take up a more prestigious coaching position. For the Emerging and Middle Leaders it was a powerful opportunity to dissect a real-life case study of a leader who professes to hold values he actually doesn't.

> **GROUNDED LEADERSHIP PRACTICE**
>
> It's time to identify your values! I recommend using Brené Brown's Dare to Lead values identification protocol, available at brenebrown.com/hubs/dare-to-lead. Brown suggests narrowing down to just two values. Many of the leaders I have worked with have found this useful advice. The exploration and journey of discovery you can go on to narrow down to two values adds great layers of depth and understanding.
>
> Brown offers three questions to help you land on your values (Brown, 2018):
>
> - Does this define me?
> - Is this who I am at my best?
> - Is this the filter I use to make hard decisions?
>
> I've also found it useful to think about what I really can't stand – situations that viscerally affect me – and from there try to determine why. Which of my core values was the situation clashing with?

Values as a guide

Defining your values allows you to engage them to guide you, especially in challenging or difficult situations. Think about a difficult time you made it through or a hard situation you handled in a way you were proud of. What helped you? What did you draw on?

Values can act as our compass, our north star guiding us. As we get intentional about this work we become familiar with what it feels like to stay aligned and what it feels like to go against or dismiss our values. We learn what it feels like to get lost, when the firm footing beneath us becomes shaky and we lose our anchor, the placeholder that keeps us from being at the mercy of the waves breaking and flowing around us.

Knowing and intentionally drawing on our values can help us to avoid 'hunting with the hounds, running with the hares' – an old saying to describe someone who switches allegiances and changes their opinions freely to suit their context and the company they keep.

Our values are significant markers of who we are, but we don't need to despair if there is some practice, value or way of being that we don't have in our toolkit just yet. This journey of mapping our sacred ground encourages us to create a toolkit of practices and to keep it alive and dynamic; to be intentional about how we show up and the ways in which we demonstrate and uphold our values and vision.

JOURNAL PROMPTS

- What does it mean to you to fully live your values as a leader?
- When have you clearly felt out of alignment? What did your body, your mind and your energy tell you?
- Did you experience any physical sensations, such as butterflies in the stomach or a closed throat?

CHAPTER FIVE

EXPLORE

Explore the human you are

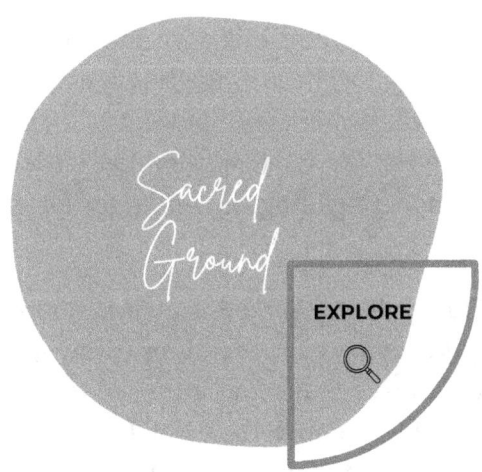

As humans with more than a handful of years behind us, we have collected and developed experiences, biases, strengths, challenges, stories and habits that have served to shape us into the people and leaders we currently are. These influences may not always be visible or memorable, but they form part of our sacred ground and their effects are present in how we show up, how we interact, our style under pressure, and the people and situations that seem to bring out the best and worst in us.

This chapter is concerned with self-awareness. We'll explore the human you currently are, and why and how you do the things you do. We'll look at things like the stories you tell yourself, your strengths, and how to identify and work through your blind spots.

In this stage of the framework, I imagine each of us sitting at our own huge mixing desk – just like the ones sound technicians use in recording studios and performances, covered in sliders, switches and buttons to manage the volume, the bass and a whole lot of other technical musical stuff I won't pretend to have knowledge of. The more we build our awareness, the greater control we have over the mix: we can dial up strengths as needed and dial down unhelpful thinking habits that may become obstacles to action or creativity.

Sound engineers don't set the mix once and then walk away; they are constantly adjusting for the setting, the acoustics and the audience. And that's what self-awareness empowers us to do as leaders: adapt, adjust and respond. The more we develop our self-awareness, the greater our chances of getting the mix right for whatever situation we are in.

In her book *Rising Strong*, Brené Brown famously said, 'When we own our story we get to write the ending' (Brown, 2015). When I first read that quote I loved it and was attracted to the idea of rewriting my story. But did you notice the error I made in comprehension? I thought I could *rewrite* my story – but it turns out that taking a big eraser to my life and rubbing out the bits I didn't like, the bits that were painful or embarrassing or shameful to remember, isn't the way it works. Nope. I've discovered that if you want to take ownership of your story, you've got to go and reread those chapters you wish weren't part of it. But that's not all. It turns out that you've also got to find a dwelling space for the excruciatingly uncomfortable feelings that are like the emotional soundtrack to those chapters.

A warning at the outset of this chapter: once you get started on the wild ride of self-discovery it can be tempting to pull at every thread, flip over every rock and take one self-assessment or diagnostic after another. Staying open to discovery and feedback is important; continuing to learn and grow is important. But beware of getting stuck in introspection. We are endlessly fascinated with ourselves and drawn to discovering insights and nuances about our personality and behaviours. But discovery alone is not enough. What we discover needs to be applied, tested, reviewed, adjusted and embodied in order to make a difference.

We also need to remember that courage and vulnerability go hand-in-hand. As such, I invite you to summon your courage and prepare to get vulnerable in this chapter. Hold yourself with compassion and kindness as you bring your blind spots – those parts of yourself you might not yet see or perhaps would prefer not to have – into the light.

The puzzle of you

One of the most powerful tools we use in the Emerging and Middle Leaders Project is the Johari Window. It's a simple but profound model that helps us understand the different ways we see ourselves, and gives us insight into how others see and experience us, too.

Developed by psychologists Joseph Luft and Harrington Ingham, the model offers four quadrants for participants to map:

- The 'open self' (what we and others know about ourselves)
- The 'hidden self' (what we know about ourselves but hide)
- The 'blind self' (what others know about us that we don't)
- The 'unknown self' (what is unknown by us and others).

Once they have created their map and analysed the data they have collected, participants typically experience some 'aha' moments.

This work is about seeing ourselves more clearly and with greater awareness, shrinking the size of our blind spots and expanding the area of what we know and understand about ourselves – because the more we see and understand about ourselves, the more choice we have in how we show up.

As one middle leader reflected as we neared the end of our work in the Explore stage of the framework: 'It's all starting to come together, the puzzle of me...'

Self-awareness

Each leader receives a journal when they begin work with me: simple in style and design, constructed of brown paper with the words *Lead Self, Lead Others* printed on the cover. I chose the slogan to remind each participant of this powerful message: leadership isn't just about leading others. It starts with understanding and managing yourself.

Emma, a participant in one of the Emerging and Middle Leaders Projects, had always believed leadership was about managing others – guiding teams, making decisions and solving problems – until she began to realise it actually started with managing herself. During her year in the project, and with her commitment to be open to new ideas and perspectives in order to grow into the leader she aspired to be, she began to see things differently. 'I wonder if self-awareness is maybe the most important thing for a leader?' she reflected as we walked out of the room for our lunch break one day. It was a statement she made simply that pointed to a profound realisation: the more she understood her own triggers, strengths and areas for growth, the more effectively she could navigate challenges and lead others to successful outcomes.

Throughout the year, Emma noticed patterns in her leadership. She had a tendency to jump to solutions before fully hearing her team members, often moving too quickly in an attempt to be efficient and get things done. Slowing down and actively listening changed everything. Emma reflected: 'I started using phrases like, "Can you tell me more... help me understand your thinking on that..." and I noticed that conversations became deeper and more productive.'

By the end of the project, Emma no longer saw her leadership as something she had to prove through how many tasks she could get completed. Instead, she approached it as a continuous process of learning – about herself and those she led.

Grounded leaders develop and highly value self-awareness. They understand that it is just one facet of emotional intelligence: the ability to understand and manage your emotions, as well as recognise and influence the emotions of those around you. The term 'emotional intelligence' was coined by researchers Peter Salovey and John Mayer (1990) and later popularised by psychologist Daniel Goleman (Landry, 2019).

Organisational psychologist Tasha Eurich and her team created an evidence-backed definition of self-awareness that is useful as a guide in mapping our sacred ground and exploration of self. But before I share it with you, let me share one of the interesting insights the team uncovered. It turns out that most of us believe we have pretty good self-awareness, yet the reality is that only a small number actually do – about 15 per cent of us, according to the team's research and definition (Eurich, 2018). So if you're sitting here thinking 'I've got pretty good self-awareness – I could probably skip over this chapter', you may want to rethink that!

Eurich's team found that self-awareness has two parts:

1. Awareness of self
2. Awareness of how others perceive/experience you.

The second point is important because, as a leader, to have an impact you need people who'll work with you, who'll support you and your vision and follow you. To get them on board, to have them feeling safe enough to enrich and strengthen the team through honest sharing, debate and challenge, you need to know how they are perceiving and experiencing you.

JOURNAL PROMPTS

- When do you feel most like yourself in leadership? What conditions allow you to lead from that grounded place?
- If you asked a trusted colleague to describe how they experience you as a leader, what do you imagine they would say? What surprises or tensions come up as you consider that?
- What's one pattern you've noticed – either in how you show up or how others respond to you – that you haven't yet explored fully?

Managing your emotions

Brené Brown calls it numbing (Brown, 2012): anything we do so we don't experience the discomfort and vulnerability of life. It might be over-eating, over-drinking, binge-watching, binge-shopping, keeping crazy-busy, over-working or any number of clever cop-outs.

For many of the clients I serve, their numbing behaviour is keeping busy. They keep doing and doing rather than slowing down to be present. One of my clients, Talia, was a classic example of this. Not only did she work all day as a specialist teacher and team leader – a role that required her to be 'on' the whole time – she'd get home in the evenings and be 'on' for her family. When Talia did make time for herself, she kept doing: she would go to the gym and run, and while she was running she listened to a podcast. She was making absolutely damn sure that *nothing* – no thought, no discomfort – was poking its way into her consciousness. When I asked her what it might be like if she simply stopped for a little while, she was aghast and truly bewildered. 'But what would I *do*?' she asked me.

I believe that it's our responsibility as leaders to be engaged in growing and deepening our self-awareness and broadening our understanding of the humans that we are. A big part of this involves uncovering and working with the tendencies, habits and thoughts we have – especially the unhelpful ones.

We all have strong emotions. If you're really honest about it, if you stay awake and aware, you'll notice your strategies and patterns for avoiding them.

Typically we don't get curious about our strong emotions. According to neuroscientist Dr Jill Bolte Taylor (2008), when we react to something in our environment there's a 90-second chemical process that happens in the body. After that, any remaining emotional response is us choosing to stay in that loop. Yet we often avoid strong feelings as soon as they arise. We don't allow the 90 seconds it takes for the chemicals of strong emotion to move through our system. We avoid the discomfort or the vulnerability because we believe that, once we are there, we might come across something we don't want to deal with.

Being in those moments can be a bit like having a mirror held up to us – one we don't want to look into. As soon as we start to feel uncomfortable we reach for our phone or open the fridge or call a friend. And here's the real kicker: we have become so good at this that we often do it unconsciously. We don't even realise the pattern we are in.

> **JOURNAL PROMPTS**
> - As a leader, are you aware of what your numbing habits are when it comes to feeling strong emotions?
> - Do you have a go-to strategy to help you when you're in those difficult situations?

The shadows

I've always feared swimming where I can't see the bottom. The dam on my brother's farm is incredibly inviting on a hot day, but I can't quite jump in with abandon. I'm always held back by worry about the creatures, forgotten fence posts or bales of old barbed wire that might be lurking in the muddy water, just waiting to do me harm.

When a place is dark and unknown it can be scary, and the colourful thoughts and technicolour images evoked by our imagination and fuelled by a deep-seated fear of what lies in the dark can be terrifying. It might seem much safer, easier and more comfortable to leave it there, unseen and unexamined.

But ask any child who has been unable to sleep for fear of monsters in the cupboard or under the bed: ignoring the imagined is not always possible. Things tucked away in dark places have a habit of showing up in some way – they leak into our subconscious and our consciousness, impacting our thoughts and our actions.

Carl Jung (1959) wrote, 'Everyone carries a shadow, and the less it is embodied in the individual's conscious life, the blacker and denser it is.' Now, with the greatest respect to Jung, that's a bit heavy for this book. I'm here to help us slow down and be grounded leaders, not be flattened on the ground by the dense weight of our unconscious! It is not my intention, nor within my expertise, to help you explore your shadow to the depth of clinical psychology. For the purposes of this book, when I say 'shadows' I am referring to our blind spots: those habits, traits and characteristics that we are not aware of, and that may be holding us back.

When we are outside in the light, we each have a shadow; and so too as humans it is normal and natural for our inner world to cast both light and shadow.

When we shine a light into the shadows, through reflection, feedback, professional support or a combination of these, we expand our awareness: things are no longer hidden. We can deepen our understanding of what makes us *us* and why we feel and act the way we do. With this awareness comes empowerment and choice.

On a trip to Mexico in 2023 we went swimming in a cenote (a natural pool formed from a sinkhole). It was idyllic: deep blue water, vines trailing down the tall sheer walls, small rocky overhangs we could swim under and, occasionally, a small school of delicate tiny fish brushing by. I lay and floated in that cenote watching the clouds pass and feeling very zen and mindful, until my brain started creating stories about how deep the water was and what offerings might have been made there centuries ago and what remains of those offerings might perhaps be down below where the water got darker!

Mexico is home to more than 4000 cenotes. The Mayan people considered cenotes the doorway to a 'mystical underworld called Xibalba, where various deities and supernatural beings resided' (Vergano, 2023), and they would throw offerings down into the deep pools – mostly precious metals and such items, but occasionally more grisly sacrifices of animal and human bodies were made.

While I've never swum in one, I have visited many of the holy wells dotted across Ireland. These are small pools, sometimes tucked beside churches, sometimes secluded in what are now farmed fields dotted with sheep and cows. These wells, wherever they sit, retain the sacred status given to them centuries ago. Even if they're on private property, members of the public retain the right to visit them. At particular times of the year a 'pattern' may be walked around the well, echoing its past as an important element in rituals and celebrations.

Irish author John O'Donohue wrote, 'wells were sacred places… threshold places between the deeper, darker unknown subterranean world and the outer world of light and form' (O'Donohue, 1997).

O'Donohue reassures us that while the Celts saw wells as doorways to the underworld they also believed that 'the underworld is not a dark world, but a world of spirit' (O'Donohue, 1997). I like this as a reframe for those parts of ourselves we'd prefer not to own or shine a light on.

What if exploring our blind spots and understanding them wasn't about uncovering darkness but about accessing the depth, richness and variety of our character? What if instead of fearing a dive into ourselves we were able to see it as an exploration of our spirit – that which gives us our spark and makes us who we are?

Sometimes, despite our best intentions, it's hard to look in the mirror. Danny, a school leader I once worked with, was frustrated by the staff at his school. He was struggling to form relationships with them and found many of them to be 'blockers' who seemed to have something negative or sceptical to say about every initiative or change he tried to bring about. Danny was sick of their resistance and had been steadily taking a stronger, more top-down approach to try to make things happen and get his staff on board.

The challenges he was experiencing in the workplace were an ongoing theme of our coaching sessions, specifically that he simply couldn't understand why the staff were so resistant. He had concluded that they didn't like his ideas or the changes he was trying to make because they were one or more of the following:

- stuck in their ways
- anti-authority
- young, inexperienced and entitled.

This collection of labels allowed Danny to categorise almost every staff member and any situation that arose.

As a coach, one of my roles is to help my client consider that there may be different possibilities, motivations and perspectives for the situations or concerns they bring to coaching to discuss and explore. Each time I had offered Danny an alternative motivation or possibility to consider, he had dismissed it, returning to the labels he had developed for the blockers and the stories he had settled on as to why things were not working. On one occasion Danny walked out of our session – unhappy with me sharing that I myself had at times found him unwilling to listen, and appearing to already have made up his mind about the concern we were discussing.

During the year, Danny had the opportunity to complete a 360 assessment. The assessment was a multipart tool that required Danny to rate himself against a comprehensive list of criteria, and he was also to invite a handful of staff members to complete a similar questionnaire on him and his leadership style and impact.

I was delighted when he told me that he had chosen to take part in the assessment, and I was hopeful that he would select a wide variety of staff who would give honest feedback that would trigger Danny's curiosity and prompt him to consider his role in the workplace culture and deteriorating relationships.

One afternoon Danny entered my coaching office ready to share with me the results of the assessment. As he opened the folder that contained his report, he prepared me for what I was about to read.

'The results are excellent,' he said. 'Everyone agrees.' He explained to me it was not a surprise to him that everyone who had contributed their own feedback had agreed with his assessment of himself and marked him highly on how he showed up and led the school. He declared how happy he was with the results and how it affirmed for him that those blockers on his staff were just whingers who needed to get over it or get out. He snapped the report folder shut and sat back with a satisfied and somewhat defiant look on his face.

I got the sense that the only contribution Danny was looking for from me was an apology for my challenges, and an acknowledgement that he had been right all along. My last hope was that the consultant who presented the results to each leader in a private interview might have stirred Danny to consider the range of possibilities his results represented. 'What did the consultant say about your results?' I asked Danny, ready to echo any concerns the consultant might have made about their homogenous nature.

'He said he'd never seen anything like them!' Danny proudly announced.

Believing in my client's capacity to grow, learn and change is essential to my effectiveness as a coach and ultimately to the progress my client makes. I had found believing in Danny increasingly difficult; I couldn't see his willingness to be open, vulnerable or curious. His participation in the 360 assessment had given me a glimmer of hope that we might be able to progress in coaching. But it did not appear to be going well.

As we sat face-to-face, report folder neatly clasped closed on the table in front of us, I wondered, was Danny willing to unsnap that report and consider it from a different angle? Was he willing and able to dial up his courage and explore the possibility that he might have a part to play in how his relationships with staff were?

It turned out that, unfortunately, he wasn't. Danny strongly rejected my invitation to consider things differently and explore the feedback that the blockers had given. Shortly afterwards, we ended our coaching agreement. I couldn't make him see or do things differently; I could only make the invitation to explore. It was up to Danny to accept the invitation.

Danny's story is a powerful reminder of how easy it is for our shadows to keep us stuck. Instead of getting curious about the feedback, he clung tightly to the stories and labels that protected him from discomfort. His unwillingness to step into vulnerability, to explore what might be less helpful or less flattering about his leadership, ultimately stalled his growth.

As leaders it's not perfection that defines us – that's never the goal. It's our willingness to lean into the hard truths when they surface, to stay open and to keep choosing growth even when it feels uncomfortable.

JOURNAL PROMPTS

- Pause your reading here – this is a big chapter! What's coming up for you?
- Is there a situation or person that might be serving as a mirror for you at the moment?

Character strengths

I first learned about character strengths through positive psychology practitioner Michelle McQuaid. I loved her explanation that our character strengths profile can serve as a hint into how our brain is wired, particularly by looking at our 'signature strengths' (those presenting as the top five strengths in the VIA Institute on Character strengths survey report).

A substantive study led by positive psychology practitioners Chris Peterson and Martin Seligman resulted in the classification of the 24 character strengths common to all humans (2004). While we possess all 24 strengths, we each have a unique combination of them, forming our individual profile. Our signature strengths tend to feel natural to us or to 'come easily', and therefore we tend to reach for them often. These signature strengths can feel so much a part of who we are that we may not even notice how often we use them. But studies have shown a wide range of wellbeing benefits as a result of applying strengths intentionally.

Inspired by Michelle, I have gone on to explore character strengths with almost every educator, leader and team I have worked with. Education is a dynamic, high-demand, often stressful profession; and with character strengths offering evidence-based, low-intervention ways to boost or protect wellbeing, why wouldn't we utilise them?

It's always fun to work with a team on strengths. I invite them to take the VIA Institute on Character strengths survey and obtain their character strengths profile. This tool and the report are a generous offering from the VIA Institute, whose work is well-researched and scientifically validated. I encourage you to seek it out if you are not familiar with it.

When I'm working with teams, we share and discuss each others' signature strengths, affirming the different ways our colleagues' strengths are evident in how they show up. Inevitably there are some 'a-ha' moments too and lots of laughing about some of the quirkier habits we have as humans.

We lean into the mixing-deck metaphor and explore what it looks like when we dial our strengths up too high. For example, people with Honesty as a signature strength can all tell a story of how their honest comments or feedback landed badly! Those with Love of Learning as a strength can get so caught up in researching, learning and going down different rabbit warrens of information that they can have difficulty getting work completed in time.

We also explore how intentionally dialling up a strength can help lift energy, motivation or connection. For example, someone with Teamwork as a signature strength might deliberately choose to co-work with others during demanding projects for the energy and positivity it brings them. Someone with Zest might commit to a morning ritual that lifts their energy before engaging in the key demands of the day. Those high in Appreciation of Beauty and Excellence might consciously seek out inspiring environments – via a walk or moment outdoors in nature, perhaps – to refresh their focus and optimism.

Importantly, we also look at the team profile of strengths. Where are we strong? Where do we have plenty of representation of strengths, and what strengths are not represented at all on our team? What are the impacts of our unique team strengths profile? What might we need to be aware of as we do our work, make decisions, meet and work on projects as a team?

Strengths clashes and challenges

It's to be expected that with a team of people who each have a unique character strengths profile, clashes will occur. That's where knowing our own strengths and those of our team members can help us to understand each other better. In the spirit of 'lead self, lead others', being aware of our own strengths can in turn help us to get better at spotting others' strengths and seeing some of their behaviours through that lens.

Kayla, a deputy principal participant in a Leadership Huddle I facilitated, shared a story that illustrates beautifully how team members' strengths can clash:

> *My top strength is Appreciation of Beauty and Excellence and I have the strength of Perspective in the top five as well. I've learned that both of these contribute to my strength as a big-picture thinker. I wish I had known about this years ago!*
>
> *I was doing a role-play exercise one day with my fellow deputies and our task was to plan a school fete. I was leading the fictional meeting, inviting discussion and trying to get the committee to make decisions on the theme of the fete, the stalls we'd have, the attractions we'd provide and so on.*
>
> *One of my deputy colleagues, playing the role of committee member, kept saying things like, 'But who's going to order that?' and 'Where will we set that up?' And it was driving me crazy. I wanted to reach across the table to her and say, 'Stop it! Stop slowing things down and getting in our way.' I was so frustrated!*
>
> *But actually, if I think about it now with my new knowledge of strengths, it's likely she had the strength of Prudence – she was great at detail, risk-management and careful planning*
>
> *With the benefit of a few years, greater emotional intelligence and, now, strengths awareness, I know that as a leader, I need that colleague on my team, because if you leave it to me and my*

big ideas, they're brilliant, they're exciting and energising, but nothing will actually happen and mistakes will occur, things will be overlooked or under-prepared, because I won't look at the detail.

And so, my colleague and I were a strengths clash, and we ended the role-play task locked in that clash, at least partly because I wasn't smart enough back then to realise that it was our strengths and perspectives that were clashing. I walked away from that task thinking, 'Gosh, she's a pain in the arse. I'm never going to go and work at her school.'

As well as demonstrating the power of strengths awareness, Kayla's story highlights what can happen if we don't shine a light on the shadows or unknown parts of ourselves, or 'make the unconscious conscious' (Jung, 1959). We create stories or dismiss others as difficult, defiant or some other label which helps us make sense of the discomfort of working with them. It happens all the time. But at what cost?

Research tells us that we do ourselves and our teams a disservice when we fail to value the full diversity of strengths within the group. In *Big Potential* (2018), Shawn Achor shares that high-performing teams aren't made up of the same kinds of people. Real strength comes from a rich mix of perspectives, energies, strengths and ways of working.

When we recognise and amplify each other's differences, we unlock far greater potential, together.

Knowing about character strengths, and being able to see strengths in ourselves and others, can help us to depersonalise clashes or heated interactions. In Kayla's case, had she been looking through a strengths perspective, she might have seen that her challenging colleague had the strength of Prudence and may have been over-playing it. If she'd recognised this, she might have been less likely to label her colleague a control freak she could not stand working with.

Interestingly, according to anecdotal data I've collected, having run the VIA Institute survey with many educators and teams of teachers over the years, a high number of us have Kindness in our top strengths – which is perhaps not surprising given that teaching is a caring profession. There is a 'shadow' of this strength, though, and you probably won't be surprised by this if you are in education: teachers tend to direct their kindness to others and find it much more difficult to turn that kindness towards themselves.

Julia, the leader of a Year 3 teaching team, wasn't surprised to read her VIA Institute strengths survey results and learn that Humour was her top strength. That tracked; she was always the one to lighten things up, crack a joke or drop a classic one-liner. Julia was funny and fun to be around, and she was proud of that.

As we explored the concept of the shadow side of our strengths, Julia was a bit surprised to discover – although I suspect that deep down she had an inkling – that humour could be overused; that it might be something she leaned on to avoid uncomfortable moments.

In between our sessions together, Julia conducted her own research project. She wanted to observe how she employed humour in her day-to-day world. Along with the typical to-be-expected moments, it became clear that humour was her go-to in uncomfortable or difficult situations. When she felt like things were getting 'a bit serious' or that the spotlight was on her for too long, Julia cracked a joke or made a humorous, self-deprecating remark to ease her discomfort and, hopefully, change the subject.

During our work together, one of Julia's team members bravely shared that when they wanted to give her a compliment and she laughed it off, they felt a bit rejected – a bit like their comment was dismissed. Julia's ears pricked up at this. She thought about how else her overplayed humour might be making her team members feel. She wanted to be a collaborative, curious leader her team could talk with honestly. She wanted rigour and debate among the team, but now she was wondering – had she been getting in the way of that?

So Julia set herself a challenge and used an Implementation Intention – a term coined by psychologist Peter Gollwitzer to describe what I call a when/then statement – to help her: *When* she felt uncomfortable and like cracking a joke, *then* she would pause and check if it was the right moment for that.

It was 'bloody hard', she told me, and it took her a long time to find the sweet spot, a place where she felt like she was being what she called 'genuinely myself – just a more intentional and aware version'.

Julia is a brave and determined woman and so she kept at it, despite the difficulty and discomfort. She grew a bit more comfortable with having the spotlight on her, she was able to stay in more difficult conversations and interestingly, so was her team – they all got better at it. During one session they reflected that their conversations seemed somehow deeper and richer. This rolled over into their relationships at work, which seemed to strengthen, and the team appeared stronger than ever.

As a human, Julia still has a wicked sense of humour, and as a leader, she doesn't hide that – she still injects humour into her work. But now, she also has the capacity to notice when she wants to use humour to deflect or avoid and she has adopted a strategy or two that help her intentionally work through that.

Knowing your own strengths and shadows is not the only dimension to consider in this Explore quadrant of the framework, but it is one valid tool, another piece of information that allows you to be empowered and to have choice and intentionality about how you show up, how you shift around those dials and sliders on the mixing desk.

The inner critic

What does your inner critic like to whisper to you? You know the one. The voice that second-guesses your decisions, tells you you're falling short, and convinces you that you should probably wait until you're more prepared, more perfect, or more 'not you' before stepping forward.

Amy Ahlers and Christine Arylo (2015) call the internalised, critical voice that tries to keep us small the 'inner mean girl'. The thing about inner critics is that they tend to play the same old tune over and over again. We need to learn to hear that tune – and then to change the station.

> **GROUNDED LEADERSHIP PRACTICE**
>
> In his book *The Whole-Brain Child* (2011), Dr Dan Siegel described how to help children deal with their emotions by using the strategy 'name it to tame it'. The idea is to explicitly name what is going on so that the brain can move out of the limbic brain response (fear) and tap back into the prefrontal cortex (executive functioning) where reasoning, creativity, planning and other such functions are 'managed'.
>
> In my experience, name it to tame it, also works really well with our inner critic. Here's how I like to use it:
>
> 1. Become aware of the story you have running in your head.
> 2. Name it to tame it. For example: 'I'm telling myself I'm not enough.'
>
> It may help to craft a when/then statement around your inner critic. This could sound like: '*When* I catch my inner critic at work, *then* I'll name the story it's telling and remind myself that it's not true and not helpful.'

But what if your inner mean girl is actually trying to help you? It was a revelation to me when I first learned that my inner critic is actually my fear speaking, and that it was trying to protect and save me. Remember, we are wired to belong; our brains are in service of our safety and survival. Doing or saying something that could potentially ostracise us or open us to ridicule, embarrassment or shame is a no-no as far as our brain is concerned. In fact, when it comes to speaking up and speaking out, our brain prefers the safer version: *staying small and staying quiet.*

On her *Magic Lessons* podcast, *New York Times* bestselling author Elizabeth Gilbert recounted a story about her inner critic. Sitting at her desk to write one day, she heard her inner critic pipe up with jibes such as, 'What are you doing here? What you wrote yesterday was crap' and 'You've written a bestseller, you'll never do better, give up now.' Gilbert had the awareness to realise these messages were the product of her inner critic – her fear, in fact – trying to protect her from shame, embarrassment, failure and ridicule. Gilbert knew if she listened to and believed that harsh inner voice she would freeze: she would not write – she would be stuck. So, she introduced a chair into her office, and now when she hears the voice begin its string of insults, she acknowledges its presence: 'I hear you,' she says. She thanks it for trying to keep her safe and then she reassures it and makes space for it: 'I've got this, you can take a seat over there.'

Mindfulness teacher Tara Brach recounted a similar story about the Buddha (yes, apparently even he suffered from self-doubt and a harsh inner critic!). The Buddha named his inner critic 'Mala' and when Mala would start speaking self-doubt or criticism or throwing shade, the Buddha would say, 'I see you, Mala. Come and have tea.'

The crucial part of both the Buddha and the Gilbert stories is that they didn't try to punish or dismiss or fight with their inner critic. They accepted its presence and made room for it. In fact, they even thanked it for coming! The thanks acknowledges that this inner critic is the voice of our fear, and is just trying to keep us safe – safe from embarrassing ourselves, safe from being 'cancelled', safe from making enemies and safe from ending up alone.

What's the consistent wisdom in these stories? Don't try to ignore, hide, repel or silence your inner critic. Get to know it, become aware of it, understand its function and name it to tame it.

To start with, I encourage you to try to catch your inner voice when you find yourself holding back from doing or saying something. What's it saying to you? And how is that in service of your safety and protection? Is your inner critic trying to stop you from making a mistake? Being mocked? Tune in, get curious and see what you can discover. And remember to acknowledge and thank it, and see what difference that makes. Can you recognise that it's your fear at work, and then give it an extra boost of courage to go on?

Tune into the warning signs your body sends you, too. These can be powerful signals that unhelpful thinking is happening or that the inner critic is firing up. Physical signals could include tense shoulders, clenched jaw, churning belly, shaky legs or thumping heartbeat. Get to know yours. What you may discover is that you have experienced your inner critic and associated warning signs for so long that you have gotten used to them and don't hear or notice them much anymore.

On a yoga retreat some years ago I wrote the following in my journal:

> *I thought I was tuned in to my inner voice – I mean, I teach this stuff! But this weekend I discovered that I was only hearing a fraction of what was going on! Since day one of the retreat I've been deeply tuned in to my inner voice and am amazed at how many versions of the 'I'm not enough' story it speaks to me.*

I'm inviting you to gently and kindly begin the work of retraining your inner voice to speak from a place of courage. Not only that, I'm cheering you on and I'm right here doing the work beside you.

JOURNAL PROMPTS

- When did you last feel yourself shrink back, stoop down or stay silent? What was your inner voice saying to you in that moment?
- What are the physical cues you tend to experience when your inner critic is active? Where do they show up in your body? Where do you feel it first?
- If you were to have a conversation with your inner critic, to thank it for trying to protect you, what would you say? What would it say back?
- Can you create a when/then plan of action for change? For example, 'When I notice my inner voice telling me to stay quiet, I will breathe deep and say, "Thanks, but I've got this."'

Exploring our strengths, being curious about how others are experiencing us and reflecting on how we experience and interact with others all contribute to making the unconscious conscious. We need objective outside feedback and help, too, to notice our blind spots – and we'll explore that in more detail in the Lead section of this book.

A professional supervisor I once worked with was what Tasha Eurich would call a wise and courageous 'loving critic'. He would listen to me complain about the way another person was irritating me or 'just not getting it', and he would gently but firmly challenge me: 'Well, what is it in them, Katrina?' He explained that often the people who irritate us most are those who represent some quality, trait or habit in ourselves that we don't love or accept.

Ouch. But he was right.

Back in my own deputy principal days, I was privileged to attend professional learning with Maggie Farrar about building relational communities. At the conclusion of one day she left us with the following challenge: 'When you go back to work, I want you to think about the person you never want to sit next to in the staffroom – the one you avoid at all costs. *They're* the ones that you should be sitting next to; they're the ones you should be spending time with, getting to know as people.'

Often the people who frustrate us the most are in some way holding up a mirror showing us parts of ourselves we'd rather not see or own.

Self-awareness isn't always comfortable. But it is necessary.

> **JOURNAL PROMPTS**
>
> - Give yourself a score out of ten in terms of where you are in relation to the leader you aspire to be.
> - Stretch it: if you gave yourself a seven, what would an eight look like?
> - What would be different at eight?
> - How can you use your strengths to get you to that eight?
>
> For example, an eight might look like having more confidence when speaking to people. How could you intentionally use your strengths to grow in that direction?

CHAPTER SIX

HONOUR

Honour the practices that help you show up

Gnamma holes are small natural wells that can be found dotted throughout the landscape of the arid areas of Western Australia. First Nations people would cover these holes with stones and leaves in an attempt to protect the quality and lifespan of the water, hoping to ensure a supply to sustain themselves and others traversing the land (Western Australian Museum, n.d.). These water sources were sacred, quietly sustaining life in a demanding landscape.

Without explicit care, the gnamma holes would be befouled or the water supply would dry up much more quickly than it should. During the gold rush of the late 1800s, the population of Western Australia nearly doubled in a few years, increasing the demands on the region's fresh water supplies. During this time of greater demand, activity and use, many of the gnamma holes were drained or polluted (Western Australian Museum, n.d.).

In the same way, our sacred ground as leaders – that place that sustains and steadies us – needs care and attention, especially when demands rise and pressure builds.

In the Honour stage of the Grounded Leadership Framework, we are focused on valuing our metaphorical gnamma holes – our sources of nourishment and sustainability as leaders. We'll get curious about how we can sustain ourselves so that we can continue to operate as the leader we aspire to be – especially in times of increased activity and high pressure.

Getting caught in 'survival mode' is a state all too familiar for educators. We tend to be in the habit of surviving until the weekend, until the end of term, sometimes just until the end of the day. Survival is not a long-term plan. So in this chapter, we'll get curious – what are the practices that can help us show up as the leader we visioned in the Decide stage?

And it's not about just showing up once – no, we are not interested in one-hit-wonders. Grounded leaders have sustainability and longevity. They have this because they build it in intentionally. This chapter is a great opportunity to fill up your toolkit with practices that can sustain you!

In this chapter I'll be inviting you to honour:

- yourself, by committing to prioritising your physical and mental health
- those you serve, by committing to honour the practices that allow you to show up as your best self.

Fill your tank

In the country town I grew up in, we relied on tank water for our daily needs. And in a house of five kids and two adults, a lot of water was needed each day! We kids probably took it for granted that we'd turn on the tap and water would come out. Most of the time, we didn't monitor how much we used or pay attention to the level of the tank or wonder where the water would keep coming from given that it hadn't rained in months. But the tank did run dry from time to time; we'd turn on the tap and a rusty-coloured trickle would struggle out – a sure sign we had reached the bottom of the tank. At the bottom of the tank dwell the dregs: the sludgy gunk and sediment that those of us who rely on tank water conveniently forget about most of the time.

When we reached the dregs as kids, whether we liked it or not, we had to pay attention to our habits. We had to go next door, bucket in hand, and ask the neighbours if we could top up from their tank. Left with just a bucket or two of fresh water, we had to prioritise and ration its use.

As humans we each have our own metaphorical tank. As we go about our day, doing, caring, decision-making, creating, serving, interacting, moving, forgiving, managing, feeling – all the things we must do as a human and a school leader – the tank depletes. This is normal and only natural. The problem emerges when we don't top up our tank. Just like the water tank of my childhood home, when we reach the bottom of the tank we're left with the dregs.

The dregs for humans include the stuff that bubbles up and becomes visible when we are running on empty – and they're not our best qualities. The dregs might look and feel like:

- Resentment ('Why am I the only one who covers extras?')
- Impatience and irritability (snapping at others, overreacting to small things)
- Blame and cynicism (seeing problems everywhere)

- Fatigue and exhaustion (low energy, struggling to focus)
- Poor sleep and stress (mind racing).

It's pretty hard to serve others from the dregs. In fact, it's just not possible to show up as the leader you aspire to be if you do not find ways to top up your tank.

And it's not just your leadership that suffers. Guess who else has to make do with the dregs? Usually your loved ones: your family at home. They get the dregs of you – and they're the people who probably least deserve it.

So, if it's normal to deplete our tank, but unhealthy and unsustainable to empty the tank and try to operate from there, what's the solution?

Topping up your tank. Replenishing.

As with so much of this work, there is no one way or right way to protect your wellbeing and ensure sustainability for yourself. There are many validated, research-backed tools and strategies for personal wellbeing. I'll share some of my favourites with you and some that come up time and again with the leaders I work with.

First and foremost, I want you to tune in to your inner wisdom. What do you know nourishes you and fills you up? What are your tank-toppers?

For me, it's nature. A walk in the bush, sitting on the beach, floating in the water, looking out my windows at the verdant green of the trees – all of these energise me.

When I can make time, I'll take a long morning, or even most of a day, to explore a bush track. But of course that sort of time is not always possible, so things like getting out into my vegetable garden and checking on how things are growing, or looking out my office window at the birds in the trees, sometimes have to suffice as my moments in nature.

As you build your toolkit of practices that top up your tank, supporting you to show up as your best self and as the leader you aspire to be, it's important that you have a varied selection. You'll want practices that you can lose yourself in all day when time allows, and others that you can fit into the smaller moments throughout a busy day.

When you find and practise small, simple, tank-filling opportunities, you are doing your present and future self a favour. Notice how those moments refresh your energy and how it can feel like a luxury to sit outside and sip a coffee.

Running on empty

A prime time for survival mode as educators is Term 4. It's a classic cycle that I would get caught in every year, and I have come to learn that many others do, too. In Term 4 I would stay up late to try to get more done, then get up early to get in to school before anyone else did in an attempt to get in front for the day (lol!). The exhaustion of totally ignoring my body's need for rest and sleep and recovery time meant I relied heavily on caffeine to get me going in the morning and keep me going throughout the day. Leaving no time for life admin meant I had no food in the house for breakfast or to take for lunch, so I'd rely on takeaway or what I could find in the staffroom fridge – and it was probably no coincidence that there was always lots of sugar and chocolate in Term 4. (I swear caffeine and sugar keep educators standing in the last months of the year.) Then at night, after a day of pushing myself, I'd arrive home exhausted, interact with my family from the very dregs of my tank, do a bit more work, numb my busy brain with a glass of wine, collapse into bed, and then rinse and repeat the next day. It sounds dire as I write that, and I feel vulnerable sharing it with you, but I've learned that so many of us are living in our own versions of that cycle.

We work in a system that demands a lot of us: assessment, data collection, individual learning plans, behaviour management plans, risk assessments, meetings, excursions, art shows, sports days, lost jumpers, PSG meetings, yard duty, not to mention our primary role of standing in front of and serving a class full of learners every day.

No wonder our tanks drain! No wonder we grind on in the hope of getting through our to-do list, perhaps even getting a bit in front!

Surge, Rest, Ready

Being an educator can feel a lot like being pounded by waves. For most of the term we're out there in the white water, being sloshed around, pulled under, rising and dipping with the tides, trying to stay upright. And then when it gets to the end of the term, we are spat out onto the shore where we lie gasping for air.

We crash onto the couch, stunned and exhausted.

That's the reality of a term in education. It's full-on, intense. And so often as educators we are simply surviving: we survive until reports are done or the swimming program is finished or until the weekend or the holidays. Some days we are just surviving until recess, lunch or the end of the day.

You know this rhythm, don't you? That push and grind and survival that gets you to the end of the term?

I use a simple model with the leaders I work with: Surge, Rest, Ready. It's not a fancy formula, but it's real – it originated on a sticky note, capturing the conversation a school leader and I were having (see figure 6.1).

Surge is the effort. The stretch. The push.

Rest and *Ready* together make for *Recovery*. You need both Rest and Ready to truly reset.

This simple model is also adaptable. You can apply it at a macro level, where the whole school term is the Surge; or at the micro level, where you consider the Surge to be a much smaller unit: maybe a week, a day or even just a meeting. When you think of it this way you can embed recovery into your rhythm as an essential part of how you show up as leader and manage your wellbeing.

Figure 6.1: Surge, Rest, Ready

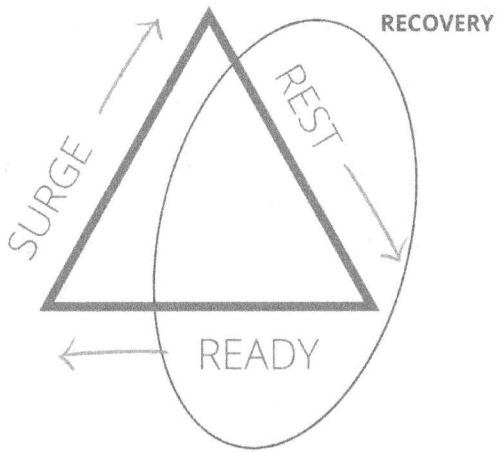

Let's take a closer look at the three parts of the model.

Surge

This is the part we know all too well. It's life as a school leader and educator: meetings, relationships, administration, planning, teaching, parent phone calls and all the other stuff you manage to squeeze into a day, including the out-of-the-blue moments you never saw coming.

There's a real energy to surging: the buzz of the school, the adrenaline of being constantly on the go, ticking through the list, moving from one focus to the next. I loved that adrenaline so much as a school leader!

Whether it's a Surge we're enjoying or one that feels more like a grind, surging takes energy. It demands something of us; it depletes our tank. So we need practices that top that tank up.

Rest

A few years ago I strained a calf muscle. It sounds mild, doesn't it? But if you've had this injury before you will know that it is not mild at all! It actually took me nearly four weeks to recover from it. I was hoping my osteopath was going to prescribe four weeks of bed rest as my recovery, but alas, it was a much more active recovery than that – I had one day of resting on the couch with my leg up, ice packs attached, but after that, I had to get moving!

At the end of term we want the full-stop, bed-rest recovery. And if you can have the bed rest, I think you should have it – for a day or two. Stay in your PJs, watch movies, switch off, eat donuts if that helps.

But then you need to get moving.

Ready

This is the bit many people skip. They think that rest is the tonic; with enough of it they should feel better.

Rest is the soother, the opportunity to calm and slow our system down. But for true, sustainable recovery, the kind that grounded leaders aspire to, you need intention and action.

Adventurers who climb mountains know this. They don't just show up at the base of Mount Everest and start climbing. They train and prepare physically, mentally and emotionally. They know it can get tough, and they anticipate and prepare for how to get through that. They have strategies for staying safe, and equipment and tools to help them achieve their goals. They even have a base camp where they can do a final preparation and acclimatisation.

In their brilliant book, *Burnout* (2019), the Nagoski sisters explain that part of dealing with your stress is to complete the stress cycle, and one of the best ways of doing that is to move your body. Not necessarily with intensity, but with intention.

So here's what I'm challenging you to do: get active as part of how you recover and rehabilitate after periods of intensity. Move your body, complete the stress cycle and give your nervous system the message that all is well.

Ready isn't just about movement – it's also about the quiet, practical things that steady you. Preparing meals for busy weeks. Looking ahead at your calendar, noticing the weeks that will ask more of you and giving yourself permission not to take on more at those times.

This isn't about chasing balance – I'm not convinced that such a thing is possible. It's about paying attention. Sometimes you'll tilt more towards work. Sometimes towards home. Grounded leaders notice early, respond with care and make small, sustaining choices that help them keep going – without losing themselves along the way.

This is not about *surviving* and *reviving*, pushing yourself to get through each moment.

This is recovery through *restoring* and *readying* – and it's just as important as resting.

> **JOURNAL PROMPTS**
>
> You know that the next term will have its surges. So ready your mind for it. Decide how you want to show up, and how you will use Rest and Ready to recover.
>
> - What do you want for yourself and for others?
> - How do you want to feel on the very last day of term?
> - If that's what you truly want, how will you show up each day?
> - What tools and strategies have you discovered that you can use at work and at home to help you surge, rest and ready?
> - What practical preparation can you do to make the surge times less intense?

Service or selfish?

Typically during the Honour quadrant we focus on self-care and self-compassion. Honouring practices related to these themes keeps us well, protects our wellbeing and helps us to show up as the leader we aspire to be – for the long term.

But there's one thing that gets in the way time and again: guilt. We feel guilty taking time for ourselves; we worry that we haven't 'done enough' or that we 'should' be giving that time to others, not indulging ourselves.

As educators, we're making a contribution to the lives and futures of the young people we work with.

As leaders, we're making a contribution to the school, the organisation, the team and the system we work in or for.

It's easy to confuse honouring ourselves with selfishness, but the research tells us something else. A commonly accepted understanding of wellbeing is both feeling good and functioning well. That doesn't mean everything is easy or that we are exempt from pressure. It means we are resourced enough – physically, mentally and emotionally – to keep showing up in a way that is sustainable and steady. In this way, caring for ourselves is not stepping away from service, it's strengthening our capacity to serve.

The PERMA framework, developed by Martin Seligman, outlines what he describes as the pillars of wellbeing:

- Positive emotion
- Engagement
- Relationships
- Meaning
- Accomplishment.

Over many years of working with school leaders and staff, I have learned that educators tend to rate their sense of Meaning quite high.

It is, after all, right there in front of them every day: the students they teach. For us as teachers, the challenge is typically not about finding meaning in our work, it's about balancing the responsibility that goes with it. We know our students so well, we see the difference our work and our input can make to them. We want so much for them to grow and achieve that it's tempting to keep giving, keep creating resources, keep planning better lessons and keep building extraordinary learning experiences and environments for them.

The same goes for us as leaders: we see the difference we can make for our colleagues and the teams we lead, so the temptation is to put in more and more to help lighten their load, help them be their best, support them to enact their vision. All of this doing and giving comes at a cost – it depletes our tank. And yet, how often do you try to squeeze more into your day? When's the last time you heard yourself say 'I'll just…'

At the risk of sharing too much information, I'll tell you about the moment when I realised how 'I'll just…' had become a problematic way of thinking for me. I was working at home juggling online meetings, preparation for upcoming workshops and trying to fit in home chores such as washing and cleaning into the cracks between tasks. As I rose from my desk to go to the bathroom, the washing machine buzzer went off, alerting me that a cycle of washing had just completed. In response, I said to myself, 'I'll just hang that out,' and headed to the clothes line with a full basket of washing. I quickly found myself hopping from foot to foot – not just delaying my visit to the bathroom, but making myself physically uncomfortable in my quest to squeeze in 'just' one more thing. Crazy!

Meaning and purpose are not just abstract concepts for educators and educational leaders – we come face-to-face with them each day in the humans we work with and serve; the humans we care about. Because of this real connection and care for people, and because we feel our work is never done and our time is never enough, it can feel selfish to stop. We can be racked with guilt about 'putting ourselves first'.

But I reckon that mindset deserves scrutiny. Are we putting ourselves first when we choose to stop working for the day or when we choose to sit down and eat lunch with our colleagues rather than holding a lunch club with students or making a phone call to a parent? I'm not sure that it's helpful to describe this as 'putting ourselves first'. Doing so contributes to either/or framing – it's me or them, it's for the kids. Many teachers and leaders I've worked with speak of feeling the constant pull of guilt as they try to juggle the myriad responsibilities and components of family and work life; feeling guilty about not working when they are with their family, then feeling guilty when they're at work after hours that they are not with their family. (Of course, they rarely factor themselves in there, and don't tend to consider how they are not giving time to themselves!)

The mental gymnastics required to figure out how to allot the finite number of hours we have in each day is real. My suggestion is that when we catch ourselves feeling selfish or guilty for considering ourselves worthy of some of those precious minutes, we remember our tanks – and that we are responsible for filling them.

This comes back to our vision for ourselves as leader – the leader and human we want to show up as, the difference we want to make in the world and the lives of those we serve. Do we want to do that from the dregs of our tank? *Can* we do it from the dregs?

Topping up our tank and caring for ourselves is not selfish; it is essential. In fact, it is an act of service. We care for ourselves so that we can be the human and leader we aspire to be. Operating in survival mode, burning ourselves out, grinding on and on – these ways of operating do not make for healthy, creative, inspiring contributions from us to our teams, our schools, our systems or our family members and friends.

And this is why, in working with the Grounded Leadership Framework, we spend so much time getting clear on the leader we aspire to be. That clear vision of how we want to show up anchors us, grounds us and gives us something to measure ourselves against that is real and values-aligned.

Consider this: does pushing yourself to keep going, keep working and do just a bit more help you to be the leader you said you wanted to be? If you go back to your vision of you as a leader, did it include getting lots of shit done each day? Or did it map out the impact and influence you'd have, the growth of people and places you'd contribute to and help to inspire? Is working 12 hours a day contributing to your vision?

For too long, educators have martyred themselves, or have been subtly shaped into martyrs by the mantras 'It's for the kids', 'We're here for the kids' and 'Students at the centre'. This has set us up for the black-and-white either/or paradigm where if what we are doing is not 'for the kids' it's wrong or selfish.

Student learning is the reason schools exist – that's for sure – but educators, teachers and co-teachers, learning assistants and leaders are the ones who make the school function. They are responsible for the rigour, depth and quality of the learning experiences that are offered and the climate and culture of the school that everyone works and learns in. We can't have students without staff, so we do everyone a disservice when we operate in an either/or paradigm. There is no either/or. There is both.

How you care for and invest in yourself will directly impact how you show up and the quality of your leadership for those you serve. Grind on and focus on getting things done and you'll probably be a pretty good manager – a good box-ticker and list-smasher. When you're focused on tasks and getting things done, people – yourself and others – don't matter so much. They become a means to an end: obstacles or enablers. And, sure, you could argue that you're getting things done for them, so that they can have an effective, safe, functioning environment to learn and work in – that's true and it's a legitimate part of your role. But it's not everything.

I worked with a team of staff who, during our time together, had a new principal appointed. This principal was proud to be a get-things-done leader. They had built their leadership identity on being someone who could come into a school, see what needed 'fixing' and get on with fixing it. The principal was proud to identify in this way.

The staff were apprehensive when they heard which principal had been appointed, but they knew there were things that needed change, abandonment or improvement and they were open to this. What they weren't prepared for was the pace: the relentless and fixed focus on 'the list' above people, above students, above what was best for the long-term plans and needs of the school community. In the first year, this principal demolished school buildings, eliminated student support programs to 'free up' funds and changed the structure of classrooms and the leadership team. The place began to look better – there was visible change and improvement to the facilities – but at the cost of staff psychological safety and wellbeing. Staff began to feel they had lost their autonomy and their opportunity to contribute to the school's direction and to advocate on behalf of the community and its unique needs. That was in large part due to the command-and-control tactics and focus on 'fixing' that the leader seemed to be driven by.

In that principal's defence, I am confident that they believed they were doing their job and making a difference for the community. Had we had the opportunity to sit down and talk about their vision and values, I'm pretty sure they would have been able to talk me through how their actions were aligned with their vision for the school and demonstrate how their values were guiding their actions. I don't believe they were setting out to do harm or to destroy people or culture. But they did.

If we zoom out and relate that principal's actions to the Grounded Leadership Framework, they were strongly placed in the Decide quadrant – with a clear vision of what they wanted to do and, perhaps, how they would show up to get that done. Unfortunately, they didn't seem to have done the emotional intelligence work contained in the Explore quadrant, nor the communication and culture-building of Lead.

Leaders have incredible power, don't they? Leaders of any industry, probably, but I know schools best, so I'll talk about my experience there.

It's my belief that with the enormous power leaders have comes a responsibility to be aware of how they wield it: knowingly and unknowingly; intentionally and unintentionally; strategically and accidentally. I believe we need more leaders who are deeply cognisant of their power and influence and are also deeply concerned with deploying that power and influence in ways that are clear, considered and compassionate.

We live in a world where, with the help of AI tools, we can generate a plan for action, have our emails and newsletters and other forms of communication written for us and have our class and school structure planned. All of these possibilities are so appealing to us as overwhelmed and time-poor humans and school leaders. Given the opportunity to outsource tasks to AI, I believe it is crucial that we make the time to be clear on our vision for our own leadership and for the community we serve. It's vital that we consider the impacts of our actions and that we act with compassion and consideration for the unique needs and circumstances of the humans in our orbit. A McCrindle research report, 'Seven Disruptors Impacting the Future of Education', stated that 'Even in the future, the most valuable skills will be distinctively human ones' (McCrindle, 2023).

In the same report, the top five answers to the question 'What qualities do you value in a leader?' were:

- Approachable
- Clear communication
- Integrity
- Empathy
- Accountability.

As AI becomes more capable, our responsibility as leaders isn't to race alongside it pursuing higher and higher levels of clever efficiency. It's to become more human. We are wise to keep up and employ the tools to our advantage. We are wiser still to remember what Maya Angelou taught: 'People will forget what you said, people will forget what you did, but people will never forget how you made them feel.'

Tools that help us plan, write, respond – and more – are fantastic additions to our kit. But they can't replace presence. They can't build trust. They can't sit courageously with the discomfort of a hard conversation, or notice the quiet signals that someone's not okay. The more we automate, the more essential it becomes to lead with awareness, empathy and care.

The future will always need people who can act with integrity. The future of leadership, especially in schools, will belong to those who can stay steady in the spinning and lead with clarity, compassion and courage.

Vision matters. Action matters. But without human-centred awareness and connection, we risk doing harm – even with the very best of intentions.

Self-compassion

Ah, self-compassion. For so many years I saw this as 'soft' and 'woo-woo' and definitely not for me!

All those years of dismissing self-compassion were actually years of dismissing my own human needs – simply operating from the neck up and ignoring the emotions, the heart and the body that resided below my ever-on brain. Needless to say, over time I built some strong and persistent habits of thinking and acting that remain some of my biggest obstacles to this day.

Kristin Neff is a masterful teacher of self-compassion. I particularly like her self-compassion assessment (selfcompassion.org) where you can get a black-and-white score and feedback on how well you 'do' self-compassion, and also access a suite of self-compassion exercises to help you build this awareness and practice.

GROUNDED LEADERSHIP PRACTICE

One of the simplest and most powerful lessons I learned from Neff's work was to ask myself the question: 'What do you need?' That question is just one component of Neff's research-informed self-compassion practice, but it's a powerful one that highlights the value of the pause.

Next time you feel overwhelmed, or you're caught in endless doing, or you feel overcome with emotions or unhelpful thoughts, pause. Breathe deeply and slowly. Ask yourself, 'What do you need?' and listen for what your inner wisdom says.

It's easy to be flippant about the question and say that what you need is a holiday or to win the lottery. Either would be welcome, but I find that typically what I need in those moments is something a little simpler and closer to home.

At first I dismissed the practice, but in one moment of overwhelm I took a deep breath, paused and asked myself the question. The answer my inner wisdom served up to me was surprising. It wasn't the advice I usually gave myself: 'To push harder' or 'More time'. Instead it was a kinder, gentler need: 'I need to stop and have a cup of tea.' In fact, I've found more often than not the response my inner wisdom serves up is usually kind and gentle: 'Sleep' or 'Rest' or 'Focus on just one thing'. I wonder what your inner wisdom would tell you?

Of course, it's one thing to receive the wisdom of self-compassion, and a completely different thing to act on it. This is where the work we've done on self-awareness in the Explore stage of the framework supports us. (Remember that each quadrant of the framework supports and enriches the others.) By knowing our stories, our habits, our tendencies, our challenges and our strengths we can be aware of what obstacles might deter or prevent us from tending to our needs.

Perfectionism

One of the most persistent obstacles I've experienced and have witnessed in almost every single one of my clients is a tendency to perfectionism. My coaching clients are typically hard-working, high-achiever, get-shit-done type leaders. They're the ones you go to because they know how to handle a crisis, work with all sorts of people, hide their emotions and soak up a lot of anxious energy. In short, my clients could run a small country – and as educators, classroom teachers and school leaders, they kind of do! These leaders are hard on themselves – super hard. They don't like to achieve less than perfection; they don't ever want to fail or fall short of the impossibly high standards they hold for themselves. To them, self-compassion, self-kindness, tending to their own needs, even asking what their needs are – well, these are all forms of 'letting themselves off the hook'.

To my clients, self-compassion is a slippery slope to letting standards fall and letting it all unravel. They've held themselves to these standards for so long; they've prided themselves on excellence and perfection as a minimum standard no matter the cost. To loosen that off, well, they can't imagine how it could be possible. I know this. I hear it again and again. I've heard myself say it and experienced it, too.

When you carry all of that responsibility and are constantly in fear of falling short, when you feel as though you are never enough and you never do enough or do it well enough, you don't want to ask yourself what you need. You can't even begin to imagine the answer, but you're pretty sure it will be immense, somewhat scary and definitely beyond your means. When you bind everything so tightly together, including your image of yourself and what a leader 'should' be, to begin to unpick that binding is terrifying.

There is no quick fix for that feeling. It takes awareness first and then continued self-compassion, continued practice of being kind and caring to yourself. Treating yourself with the same love and compassion you would, without hesitation, show to another.

Tara Brach, another woman full of deep wisdom, teaches about the Trance of Unworthiness (Brach, 2003). It's the feeling of never being enough. She says that when we awake from that trance and realise how tightly bound we've been, how unkind to ourselves, the danger is that we berate ourselves, admonish ourselves for being so foolish and unaware. Brach's suggestion? Self-compassion.

Grit, grace, grind

When I talked with my colleague Meg Durham on her School of Wellbeing podcast we explored the idea of grit and grace, and how we can strike a balance between perseverance (grit) and self-compassion (grace).

I've thought a lot about that conversation with Meg. Our contention was a good one – find the sweet spot between grit and grace – but in my personal experience, and what I observe in the leaders I work with, we typically adopt a third option: grind. Let's take a look at all three of these.

Grit

We celebrate grit as a capability. It's the ability to persevere, to be resilient, to show up even when it's hard. Grit helps us get things done, achieve goals and move forward.

It sounds like: 'Keep going, you're nearly there.' 'You've got this.' 'It's hard, but you can do it.'

Grind

This is grit overdone. It is characterised by harshness and punishing perseverance. It's pushing on when we're too tired, or when the solution is just not appearing; making ourselves keep going because we think we 'should' or out of obligation.

It sounds like: 'Push through, no excuses.' 'Stop complaining, suck it up and get it done.' 'What's wrong with you?'

When we stay in grind mode, we just keep pushing. We don't pause or reflect, and that's where burnout, exhaustion and resentment find their way in.

The irony for us as educators is that we wouldn't treat our students like this. We wouldn't tell them to 'Work harder!' or point out all the ways they're getting things wrong. We meet our students with encouragement, kindness, helpful feedback and support. And yet, as leaders, we seem to find it difficult to apply the same sentiment to ourselves.

This is where grace comes in.

Grace

Grace is discernment. It's knowing when to rest and when to keep going, when we can demand more of ourselves and when to say 'that's enough for now'.

Grace is:

- Giving yourself permission to pause
- Allowing less-than-perfect to be good enough
- Seeking help instead of carrying the load yourself
- Acknowledging your gains, not just the gaps (Sullivan & Hardy, 2021).

Grit and grace are both essential elements of the toolkit we are constructing in Honour. The key is to be able to use them intelligently.

> **JOURNAL PROMPTS**
>
> The next time you feel yourself pushing beyond what's sustainable, ask:
> - Is this grit or grind?
> - Would I speak to a student or a colleague this way?
> - What would it look like to lean more into grace here?

Boundaries

Oh, this is a hot topic! Saying no, switching off: two of the biggest challenges I hear educators and school leaders name, time and time again.

There are a couple of obstacles that tend to cause pain and frustration in this space:

1. Not wanting to upset or hurt others.
2. Fear over when the work will get done if we switch off.

Lets take a look at each of these.

'I can't upset them'

Have you seen that meme that says, 'No is a complete sentence'? It's a goodie and it highlights what so many of us tend to do: we don't directly say no, we beat around the bush, saying things like 'I'll see if I can', 'Maybe', 'Yes of course' or 'I'll try'. We say such things despite internally kicking ourselves and wondering why we can't just say 'No' and how on earth we'll ever be able to find the time and energy to do the thing we just agreed to.

Typically what we need to make clear is our boundaries: what's okay and what's not okay. So often we keep quiet for fear of harming a relationship or out of concern for the other. We don't want to upset them or add more to their plate, or put them out – so we put ourselves out. We stay quiet, while inside us the resentment, frustration and stories of blame build. As school staff we are overloaded with work and we are highly conscious of putting extra workload on our colleagues, so often we keep quiet and keep adding to our own list of tasks.

'I have work to do'

It's very human to cross our own boundaries in order to try to get 'just one more thing done'. We tend to do this when we are engaged in the futile battle with time and our to-do list, believing that if we just work a bit harder, a bit earlier and a bit later, we'll eventually get everything done and we'll be in front. Let me break it to you bluntly: You. Will. Not. Empty. Your. To-do list. Once you make peace with that, you can stop pouring energy into trying to find the magic-bullet time and productivity hack.

> **GROUNDED LEADERSHIP PRACTICE**
>
> Take a moment to do this exercise, just the way we do it in workshops.
>
> First: draw three circles on your page. Label one *Control*, the next *Influence* and the third *No Control*.
>
> Next: brain dump! What's on your mind? Drop all the worries, tasks and stressors that are swirling around your head into the circles according to whether you have control, influence or no control over them.
>
> In Stoic philosophy, this exercise is known as the dichotomy of control. Stoic philosopher Epictetus summed up the concept memorably:

> *Happiness and freedom begin with a clear understanding of one principle: Some things are within our control, and some things are not.*
> *(Schaffner, 2023)*
>
> Take a look at your completed circles. What do you notice? What became clearer for you? Have you been focusing too much energy on things you can't control? What within your Control circle can you take ownership of? What is your next step?

Often after doing this exercise people will realise they've been focusing a lot of time and energy on things beyond their control. Another common realisation is that items within the Control and Influence circles are usually limited to our own words and actions.

I once ran into a deputy principal some years after we had last worked together. He shared with me that the 'in my control/beyond my control' concept had become a filter system for him. He said that he would pass everything that came towards him in a day through that filter. If it turned out to be something he had no control or influence over, he would try to set it aside (note, he often had to do this repeatedly with the same thing – some things are beyond our control but still very powerful at taking up headspace). If something was within his circle of influence or control he'd make a plan to deal with it. I was so delighted to hear him explain how this approach to all the spinning he encountered in a day allowed him to get a good night's sleep most nights.

The reality of workload

The amount of work that is demanded of us by our leaders, systems and organisations is often largely out of our control. We may or may not be able to have a great deal of influence over it. The more time we spend worrying about this, getting frustrated and resentful about it, the bigger and uglier and more frustrating it gets. A better use of our time and energy is to focus on those things we do have control over.

But please, do not hear me saying that you should just 'get over it' or lie down and take it. Acceptance of the demanding nature of the role is one thing. One principal told me that acceptance is what allows him to turn up to work each day. As he explained it, 'It's tough when you talk to your friends and colleagues in leadership and they can't reassure you that it will get better. There are periods of calm and progress and pride, but equally frustration, stress and overwhelm are part of the role. Once you accept this, you stop fighting against something out of your control, wishing it was somehow better or different, and allow yourself to get on with the job.'

Teacher and leader workload in education is concerning. There is plenty of available data that outlines the troubling state of principal wellbeing, teacher stress and overall job satisfaction. Workload is just one factor, but it is a significant contributor. The 2024 Australian Principal Occupational Health, Safety and Wellbeing Survey conducted by the Australian Catholic University (Riley et al., 2024) provides critical insights into the challenges faced by school leaders:

- Workload topped the list of concerns across all school types and contexts.
- Over half of respondents (53 per cent) reported an intention to leave the profession.
- Nearly half of respondents (45 per cent) triggered a 'red flag' indicating serious risk of burnout, self-harm or mental health crisis.

We must speak up about this. We must continue advocating for ourselves and our colleagues. At the very least, as grounded leaders we must find ways to do meaningful work while protecting our own wellbeing.

When we focus on things within our circle of control, our focus shifts, and we notice the impact on our attitude, wellbeing and state of mind. Schaffner (2023) cited Rohleder and Chen who found that 'the circle of control is a useful cognitive tool for individuals to manage their emotional reactions to stressful situations'; and Robertson, who wrote, 'By focusing on what we can control, we can develop a sense of inner calm and resilience that helps us to cope with the challenges of life.'

Boundaries and blame

In times of uncertainty, vulnerability and discomfort it is so tempting to find someone to blame. Finding out whose 'fault' it is gives us a semblance of control. And as humans, in situations that seem very much out of our control, we want to feel some certainty and agency.

Brené Brown's research tells us that 'Blame is… the discharging of discomfort and pain' and that it 'has an inverse relationship to accountability' (Brown, 2013).

Anyone who's been brave enough to hold themselves or someone else accountable knows from experience that accountability is a vulnerable process. Speaking clearly to someone about how their words or actions impacted you is uncomfortable.

It takes courage and grit to establish clear boundaries and expectations and to stick with them. It's so much easier to blame others for expecting too much, emailing too late at night, or not doing their share of the workload. It's so much easier to seethe silently than to speak clearly to them about your expectations and boundaries.

I'm not blaming you for blaming; I'm encouraging you to be aware of your tendency to blame and when you catch yourself, to pause and reset.

GROUNDED LEADERSHIP PRACTICE

Take some time to work out what is causing you pain or discomfort that you're perhaps blaming others for. Then approach any concerns or problems through accountability by considering the following questions:

- What do I need to make clear here?
- Who do I need to be clear with?
- How will I communicate, as one human to another, with compassion and kindness?

Insider, outsiders and offsiders

Leadership is not a solitary endeavour. By its very definition, a leader can't lead if there is no-one following!

But leaders can often feel alone. School leaders who work with me in coaching often remark that they appreciate the opportunity to speak aloud about what is on their mind, in a safe and confidential space. There are some things principals don't or can't or won't share with their colleagues, even their right-hand people, their deputies. One principal explained it to me like this: 'I don't want to talk to my deputy about this; there is nothing to be served for them from hearing it, there is nothing they can do about it, and I do not want to burden them or add to their stress.' Whether you agree or disagree with the principal's reasoning, it is a heavy burden to shoulder alone.

How can we as leaders share the load? How can we distribute the burden we carry?

In our home we have a framed series of six photos on our wall, taken by me many years ago and still in their original frame – a kind of yellow-coloured pine that was bang on trend back when I had it framed maybe 20 years ago. I still clearly remember taking the shots, standing up at the Christ the King lookout in the magnificent and scenic Glen of Aherlow in County Tipperary, pointing my camera out across the Galtee Mountains and down along the valley. Of course, 20 years ago cameras did not have the panorama feature that our phone cameras now offer, so I had to point and click along the whole mountain range, going carefully, section by section, hoping that it would all join up okay when I got home and had the photos printed.

More recently, I've been back to that scenic lookout, with better equipment including a tripod for my camera. The tripod brought stability, focus and precision to my shots, allowing me to capture a much higher-quality, clearer image.

Leadership is like that. Alone, our view can be somewhat limited; but with the right support system – our leadership tripod of insiders, outsiders and offsiders – we can gain stability and perspective around our work and our experience as leaders.

Insider

The first layer of support starts with you. The work we've outlined so far in the book, the framework quadrants of Decide, Explore and Honour, are largely undertaken by, reflected on and revisited by you. These things are within your circle of control and are your choice and responsibility to attend to. The role of the insider is to make time for self-care and reflection, make the choice to be self-compassionate, stay aligned to your values and vision, and seek professional support for your ongoing growth. When you're attending to those things you are doing your bit towards being the leader you aspire to be.

Offsiders

These are your 'peeps'. They get you and the work you do, the system you work within and the challenges you face and grapple with. Many of them are school leaders just like you. They face similar concerns and challenges, they work in the system and experience the same demands, and some of the same frustrations and resentments. Your offsiders are the ones you can contact when you need some advice, when you have a question, when you need to vent or have a 'recreational whinge', as my colleague Daniela Falecki of Teacher Wellbeing calls it. They are the people in the trenches with you, and they will support you, commiserate with you, encourage, boost and bolster you when you're worried or frustrated, upset or hurt. They'll celebrate with you when things go right, too! You don't need a lot of offsiders, but having some in your corner gives you strength, sustainability, connection, wisdom and collegiality.

Offsiders are crucial, but like so much, we must ensure we balance them and the special blend of support they offer us. That's where outsiders come in…

Outsiders

Outsiders are our sages, our mentors and our guides-on-the-side. They are far enough out of our realm that they can offer more objective support. We need to choose them carefully; we don't want to be damaged at our most vulnerable moments, so we need people with the right blend of compassion, wisdom, self-awareness and honesty who can hold a mirror up to help us see ourselves and our blind spots more fully. Our outsiders must be worthy and trusted to step carefully on our sacred ground rather than trample all over it.

Outsiders are what Tasha Eurich calls your loving critics (Eurich, 2018). They bring objectivity, balance and challenge to you, and they're not afraid to hold up a mirror to help you reflect on your role and responsibilities and how you're showing up. They are compassionate and truthful and want the best for you.

The combination of these three layers of support – insider, offsiders and outsiders – gives you depth and quality as a leader. They contribute to your wellbeing and ensure you keep a healthy perspective on your work and how you lead and interact with others.

Dr Polly McGee reminds us 'It's so important in contemporary leadership for us to be able to say I made a mistake or I don't feel confident about this or ask for help' (McGee, n.d.). Having a steadying 'tripod of support' can give us the courage and grounding to speak up in such a way and, in practical terms, ensure we have a selection of people who can give us the help we need.

> **JOURNAL PROMPTS**
> - Who are your offsiders – the ones in the trenches with you?
> - Who are your outsiders – the ones who challenge and guide you?
> - Are there any gaps in your tripod of support?

Creating your toolkit

Over time I've come to realise that our ability to recover and to remain steady, to keep going in a healthy way, isn't just dependent upon having the right tool in our toolkit at the right moment. Rather, it's an accumulation of all the self-care strategies we have in place, plus the gifts and wisdom that come from self-awareness and doing the work to know ourselves, understand ourselves and lead ourselves.

The gift of awareness gives us the opportunity to choose how we respond, to anticipate our needs and our possible reactions to people and situations and to take actions that allow us to show up as our best selves, and to reset when things don't go as planned.

Perhaps the last word in this Honour section could go to some of the wonderful people in my Grounded community. In my weekly newsletter a few years ago I asked readers for their strategies that sustain them and help them top up their tank. Here are a handful of their responses:

- I have learned to step back a bit and not to react when my anxieties are high.
- I try to see things from a different perspective.

- I try to be generous and think about what might be going on for the other person.
- Rest is an important bounce-back strategy for me – I don't operate well when I'm tired.
- Pursuing my own hobbies allows me to top up my tank and be ready to face challenges as they arise.
- Exercise.
- Yoga.
- Walk in nature, see some green trees.
- Sleep.
- Journalling.
- Breathing out slowly before responding.
- Being aware of when I'm under a brain hijack.

The challenge isn't finding the strategies – I reckon you probably already know what sustains you. Perhaps you share the same challenge as the principal who told me, 'I don't need more strategies, I have plenty, it's sticking to them that's the problem.'

It's not the number of strategies that you collect, it's about applying them, especially when things are busy and spinning fast. As my friend Liz has said to me on more than one occasion: when you don't have time to meditate for ten minutes, it's a sure sign that you really need to meditate for an hour.

And that's the work of Honour: carving out time and fiercely, bravely, assuredly protecting it. Do that and you'll find your feet. Again and again.

JOURNAL PROMPTS

Throughout the chapter we've explored how we can honour ourselves, our energy and our boundaries by:

- Establishing and upholding boundaries
- Practising self-compassion
- Intentionally recovering
- Topping up our tanks
- Building a support system.

Ask yourself:

- Which of these areas are you doing well with?
- Which would you like to strengthen?
- What's one next step you could take to make change or improvement in one area?

CHAPTER SEVEN

LEAD

Lead the way and make things happen

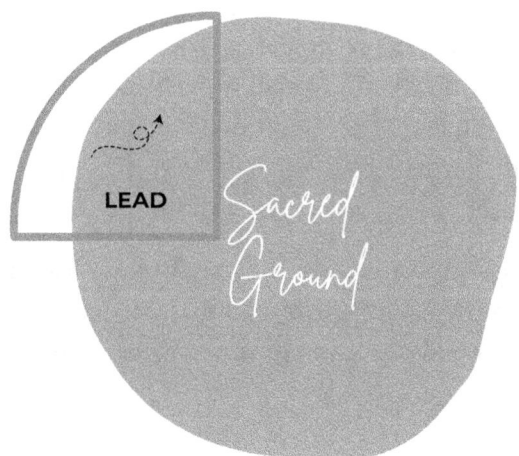

To lead is to show up as the best version of yourself and encourage and inspire others to do the same.

A lofty goal, isn't it?

This quadrant of the Grounded Leadership Framework is about action. We've decided on the leader we aspire to be. We've explored some of the traits, habits and strengths that make us the human we are. We've identified some of the practices and tools that will support us to be the leader we dream of being. All of that is vital; and yet, without applying and activating it, it's just a personal journey of self-discovery and growth.

Lead is about bringing it all together. It's authenticity in action – knowing your vision, knowing your strengths and shadows, doing your own work and mapping that sacred ground to be the leader you aspire to be.

It's also about the impact you have on others and the legacy you leave. To lead is to look outside of yourself, to be concerned with improving things, and helping others rise and have their own impact.

Throughout the book we've considered just how complex and challenging it can be to be a leader. And yet it's also fulfilling and energising, captivating, hopeful and inspiring.

In this chapter you can expect to consider how you lead. What are the conditions that allow you to be an impactful leader, and how do you create them? What are the conditions that allow those you work with and serve to rise and to have their own impact? How do you help to create those?

We'll explore communication, leading with curiosity and service. We'll look at bringing it all together – all that you have learned about your strengths and shadows – and how to harness that knowledge to empower you as a leader.

Communication

So many of the challenges and frustrations we face as leaders can be traced back to communication. Whether it's giving feedback, addressing performance concerns, advocating for change or simply managing everyday misunderstandings, how we communicate matters.

When it comes to challenging conversations, the top two obstacles I hear from educators are that:

1. They 'don't like conflict'.
2. They don't want to 'damage the relationship'.

So many of us believe that courageous, assertive conversations are conflict or are bound to end in conflict. This does not have to be the case. Further, when we choose not to raise our concerns with a colleague, we are not giving them an opportunity to become aware that we have the concern in the first place. This means we're denying them the chance to respond or to make adjustments where relevant. We are making choices for them and assuming we know what their response will be. How would you feel if someone did this to you?

Brené Brown's phrase 'Clear is kind' (2018) is a terrific mantra to keep in mind when it comes to communication. It's kind to be clear and upfront; to talk to the person involved directly rather than complaining about them to others. It's kind to listen with intention. It's kind to believe that they are capable of making any necessary changes to their actions or the situation.

Reframing it in this way can help us to see clear and candid communication as a leadership necessity. If we believe our role as leader is to encourage others and create the conditions for them to be at their best, withholding information in the hope of avoiding conflict, crossing our fingers that things will get better, or staying silent to 'protect' the other person or our relationship does not make sense.

How to have a courageous conversation

What to say and how to say it is another obstacle leaders raise with me. I love to collect sentence starters that can help. My mentor Matt, who is a renowned public speaker, says that when it comes to speaking on stage, 'state matters more than script'. In other words, how you show up, how you interact and how you present matters more and impacts more than getting the script exactly right. In my opinion the same applies when it comes to courageous conversations.

No matter how prepared we are, humans don't run to a script; and when things get off track during a conversation we have carefully planned and rehearsed, it can feel uncomfortable and we can fumble our words. If we remember 'state over script', and rather than focusing on trying to remember the exact line we had prepared, stay present and remain curious, we are sending signals to our partner in conversation that we are there with genuine intent, even if our words or delivery are a bit messy.

It pays to remember that what they say and how they react is outside of our circle of control. What we say, how we show up, how we listen and our body language all have impact, and they are all within our circle of control. Our aim should be to stay present, manage our emotions, listen to learn and to respectfully and calmly raise our concerns without blaming and in a way that is concerned with finding a solution.

It can be helpful to have sentence starters or frameworks to kick things off or help you stay on track. The FEEL framework, pictured in figure 7.1, is a simple yet effective one I like to use.

Other great resources include:

- Crucial Conversations STATE framework
- The Center for Nonviolent Communication
- Brené Brown's 'rumble starters' from her book *Dare to Lead*
- Open-to-learning conversations.

In their book *Crucial Conversations*, Grenny et al. (2012) define these conversations as those where the 'stakes are high, opinions differ and emotions run high'. This definition encompasses so many of the conversations we have in the course of a day in a school!

Grenny et al's book is a great one to read. It will help you learn to navigate crucial conversations successfully, keep relationships intact, communicate clearly and remain focused on finding meaning and solutions.

In the following pages I'll focus on some of the strategies and surrounding supports for creating and nurturing conditions that allow for honest, robust, respectful communication.

Figure 7.1: The FEEL framework

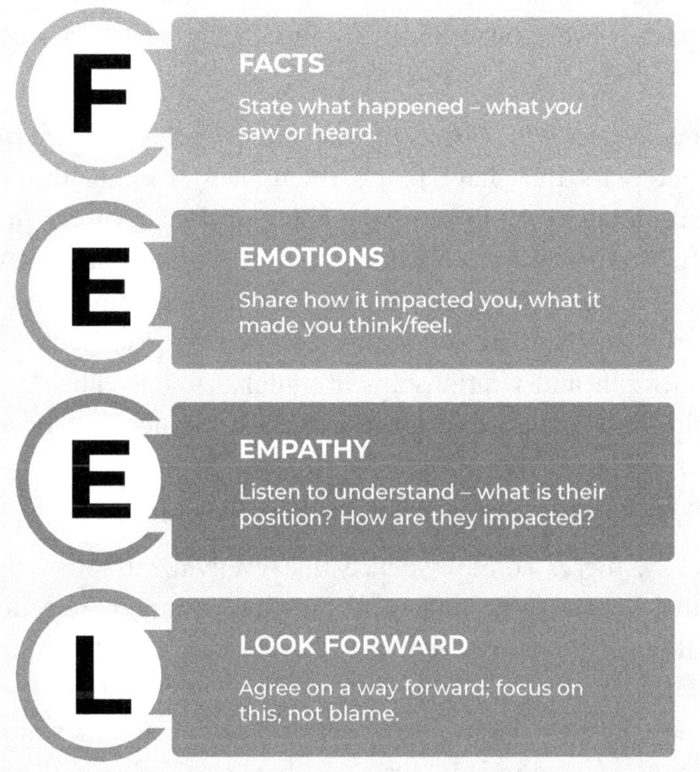

F — FACTS
State what happened – what *you* saw or heard.

E — EMOTIONS
Share how it impacted you, what it made you think/feel.

E — EMPATHY
Listen to understand – what is their position? How are they impacted?

L — LOOK FORWARD
Agree on a way forward; focus on this, not blame.

Get connected

Our human brain considers us safe when we are in connection and relationship with others. Being connected helps to avoid some potential miscommunication problems before they arise. Make time to connect with the people you work with. Get to know something about them. Sounds simple, doesn't it? Yet, think about how often in the fast pace of school life we greet each other with a quick (albeit genuine) 'How are you?', but we don't pause to listen to the reply. Sometimes we don't even expect one.

Almost everything we need in our work as educators is on our phone or our laptop, so they are usually open and drawing our attention in meetings, in the classroom and in between. We all know what it feels like when someone is not paying attention to us – when they're distracted by their screen. Others know it and feel it when you do it to them. Of course, we don't do it with the deliberate intention to harm – we're busy, and we're just trying to be efficient and get things done.

Many leaders and classroom teachers have shared with me that in recent years they have found themselves working through their break times to try to deal with their workload, rather than going to the staffroom for a break and a chat. I understand the desire to get work done at work so we have less to take home, yet this trend worries me. Humans are at the heart of our organisations. Human connection and relationships are vital to our wellbeing, and our brains and bodies need a break. Take a moment to consider how often you are making time to be with people for your own wellbeing and for the sake of your relationships and connection with others.

Luckily, there's some evidence that even in our busy, fast-paced school lives, we can build and nurture genuine connections. Jane Dutton (2003) has studied what she calls 'high-quality connections'. She found that 'any point of contact with another person can potentially be a high-quality connection'. Even small interactions are powerful – they build relationships and 'help people feel alive'. This means that, as school leaders and educators. we can make a connection as we hand over on yard duty, stand at the printer, fill our mug at the hot water tap, and sit in meeting rooms before team meetings and planning sessions begin. Taking the time to connect with your colleagues in these small moments shows that you value the other person, and helps you learn a bit about each other.

Here's how to make your connections high quality:

- **Be present:** Turn away from your laptop/phone/paper.
- **Be genuine:** We all know when someone is faking it!

- **Be affirming:** Look for the good and positive – and acknowledge it!
- **Listen actively:** Stay focused, remain curious.

Positive intent

When we are tired and busy, managing life admin, workload and whatever else might come our way in the course of a day, it's easy to get caught in a misunderstanding and for it to escalate quickly.

Being committed to positive intent means that we listen with the assumption that our colleagues do not mean offence or harm. We give them the benefit of the doubt. We start there, and then we listen to understand, we ask questions and we stay curious. Imagine the world if we all did that, even just some of the time! Again, what your colleagues say and how they react is outside of your control. So focus on you. How will you show up to these conversations? How will you address any concerns that arise?

In episode 136 of her *Making Positive Psychology Work* podcast series, Michelle McQuaid and her guest, Jon Berghoff, discuss the invite-and-inquire approach to leadership.

McQuaid explained that the invite-and-inquire approach 'comes from a place of humility and a willingness to step into your interactions with an authentic intention to listen, learn and understand where others are coming from and what alternative answers might arise to what you're facing, rather than showing up with the goal of convincing others of your opinion'.

Jacinda Ardern, former New Zealand prime minister, is an invite-and-inquire leader. One of her first actions after a violent attack at a mosque in Christchurch was to inquire: she asked Muslim community leaders, 'What do you need?' It was a simple question, but a courageous one. To inquire is to show vulnerability, a willingness to learn and an open admission that you do not know everything.

It's worth noting that not only did Arden invite and inquire, but she also led with humanity and compassion, embracing one of the grieving members of the community. This garnered plenty of attention in the media and opinion pieces on the 'correctness' of such a gesture by the prime minister.

We need invite-and-inquire leaders who have the courage to be vulnerable, who have a clear vision to guide them and to share with others. We need invite-and-inquire leaders who are not too important to roll their sleeves up and lead the way practically, and who have the guts to call out behaviours and actions that are unacceptable and offensive.

We need invite-and-inquire leaders who know their own sacred ground and who can stand and lead from that spot, especially when the going gets tough. Ardern proved herself to be such through her actions and her words: 'I refuse to believe that you cannot be both compassionate and strong.'

JOURNAL PROMPTS

- In what ways do you demonstrate an invite-and-inquire approach?
- Where are there opportunities for you to create high-quality connections with others?

How are you complicit?

It's all very well to talk about being present and intentional about how you show up and interact. But back when I was a crazy-busy deputy principal, spinning all the plates and keeping everything under control, I would have said, 'It must be nice to be present, but who the hell has time for that?'

In her podcast *We Can Do Hard Things*, Glennon Doyle explained how, when she hears herself using the phrase 'It must be nice…', she stops to investigate what's really going on in her head. What is the story she is telling herself? What is she really feeling?

I remember watching my colleagues go for lunch one day. They walked past me where I was sitting in the office covering lunchtime first aid duty, answering the phones and trying to complete the planning for a meeting later that day. As they walked past, with barely a glance at me, I saw red! 'Must be nice to just skip out for lunch without a care in the world' was what flashed across my mind. That's resentment right there. I resented their carefree attitude and the fact that they were going to eat lunch when I knew I'd probably grab a biscuit from the barrel with my next cup of coffee.

When I think 'It must be nice…' it's an indicator that I am overloaded and resentment is rising. I've developed a simple but effective formula – 'when, then' – for coming back to my sacred ground when I find myself in this state:

- **When** I notice resentment rising,
- **Then** I check my part in the situation. (I ask myself, 'How am I complicit?')

Jerry Colonna introduced me to this question, and it has become one of my favourites for myself and for my coaching toolkit. 'How am I complicit in creating the conditions I say I don't want?'

This question is not about shaming. Rather, when we identify our part in a situation, we are identifying areas that are within our circle of control – the things we can actually do something about.

In the example of my resentment at my colleagues going to lunch, how was I complicit in creating the conditions I said I didn't want? To quote the great Shakespeare: 'Oh, let me count the ways'. I was caught in a pretty unhealthy, unhelpful cycle:

- I had no boundaries, which meant I was saying 'yes' to way too much.
- Saying 'yes' to way too much meant I couldn't possibly do everything on my list, so I'd stay up late and get up early.

- I was tired!
- Jamming my days with doing all the things meant no time left for me.
- I had no time to prepare healthy food or even a healthy dinner I could take for lunch the next day.
- I had no time to go out and get something to eat.

So what did I do about it? The honest answer is that it took me a while (read: years!) to see what I was doing here. Not just the choices and actions, but the belief I was operating from. I was driven by 'not enough', specifically my fear that I was not a good enough or experienced enough leader; so in my actions I had tried to prove just how 'enough' I was, by being all things to all people and being available. Always.

Once I came to see this hidden belief and how I was creating suffering for myself, I was able to honour the practices I needed to help me show up as the leader I really wanted to be. I made time to slow down and savour small tank-filling moments such as drinking a cup of tea and feeling sunshine on my back. I committed to bigger, more practical actions too, ones that were a bit harder to build into habits: shopping for and preparing nutritious food, prioritising sleep and learning to be okay with doing almost nothing – i.e. resting.

That question 'How am I complicit?' helped me to stop spinning, to slow down and find a way forward. It still does.

Show up to serve, not to prove

There are so many ways to lead; so many ways to help others grow and become their best selves. Here's what I think is at the heart of it: it's not what we say or offer or share that matters most. It's how we show up.

When we lead from fear, we tilt into performance.

When we lead from grounded confidence, we are in service.

When we're leading others, whether it's in a meeting, a workshop, a planning session or a coaching conversation, we need to pay attention to what's going on inside of us:

- What's our mindset?
- What's our inner voice saying to us?
- What's propelling and motivating us? Is it fear, or is it grounded confidence?

When we let our fear drive, we try to prove ourselves. We are worried we are not enough: not doing enough, not providing enough, not innovative enough, not clear enough. That's about 'hustling for our worth', as Brené Brown calls it. And until we have come to know, build and trust our sacred ground, we will keep on doing it.

Another question I often return to is this: 'Am I serving or am I seeking?' When we serve, we focus on what's useful and what's needed. When we seek, we shift into performance. We flood the space. We interrupt or don't allow the moment. We make it about us, often without meaning to.

Imagine a restaurant server. A good one doesn't bring you what they think you should have. They ask, they listen, they check in. They allow space for you to choose. They don't hover or interrupt the conversation every five minutes.

The same goes for leadership.

We don't need to serve up perfect content, beautifully plated and timed. We don't need to anticipate every need and question. It's our job to create the conditions where people can reflect, engage, explore and grow. This is how we serve, not prove.

Building the habit of grounded leadership

If you catch yourself in not-enough thinking, feeling fear and the urge to perform, please don't double down and berate or scold yourself. Instead, use it as a cue to pause and get grounded.

Here's a practice we've been building throughout this book:

1. **Notice:** 'I'm performing, I'm trying to prove my worth. I'm focused on me.'
2. **Steady:** Take a low, slow breath. Come back to your sacred ground. Decide how you want to show up.
3. **Proceed:** Push your hair off your face. Step forward as the leader you aspire to be.

Nearly every workshop or session I lead reinforces these lessons to me. Perhaps the most powerful examples have been during the Leadership Huddles I run. In the huddles, leadership teams from a range of schools come together to work through the Grounded Leadership Framework in a calm, offsite, uninterrupted space. I learned very quickly that simply being in that space has value for the teams: having uninterrupted, un-rushed and focused time to connect, discuss, clarify and do deep work is something educators appreciate and are eager to make the most of. I've discovered that what participants need from me in these huddles is not a lot of content or tinkering. They need quality provocation, some personalised coaching, and space. In other words, part of my job is to stay out of their way!

The truth is, people don't need more content. They need space to think, reflect, wonder and connect.

When we lead from performance, scarcity or not enough, we fill the space.

When we lead from service, courage and vulnerability, we hold the space. And that is where growth and learning happens, for them and for us.

JOURNAL PROMPTS

There are so many ways you can lead from service. When you are leading others:

- What's your mindset?
- What's your inner voice saying?
- What's propelling and motivating you? Is it fear or is it grounded confidence?

CONCLUSION

Leadership is an evolution.

Professor Herminia Ibarra says that 'authenticity is an evolution' and 'you don't have to be who you've always been'. If we agree with this, then working on how we show up becomes exciting and filled with possibility!

There is great permission in Ibarra's words – permission to change, to grow, to evolve as a human and leader.

But growth also brings discomfort. We need our own reflective practice to check our progress and consider how we handle challenges and significant events, as well as how we show up day to day. Reflecting on what is going on inside is something only we can do. But we can't just rely on our own opinion about how we are showing up. Information on how we come across – the impact we have on individuals and outcomes – is most useful when it comes from others. Our job is to be courageous enough to ask, and wise enough to genuinely listen to understand.

And so we have come full circle: the whole point of the Grounded Leadership Framework, of exploring and understanding who you are and how you show up, is to give you the grounded confidence and courage to stand on your sacred ground and lead as your authentic self.

If you don't feel particularly courageous, or you worry that you get too nervous around others to show up authentically and courageously, don't worry. As you continue to uncover your strengths and shadows, as you gather evidence of how you are absolutely enough to lead, and as you listen to the feedback you receive from trusted others, you'll learn about yourself. You'll come to understand yourself more deeply, and you'll develop the courage to lean in to that. You'll find the conviction of knowing that others *need* you to show up as your unique self. With this awareness, you'll be in the driver's seat.

How you show up won't suit everyone. It won't always be popular or align with others' advice or opinions. That's okay. In fact, if you do suit everyone – if everyone finds you agreeable and is fully on board with all your ideas – I suggest you are not showing up authentically. You are holding back, hoping to avoid conflict or disagreement.

A memorable and thrilling moment for me was when one of my favourite leadership teachers responded to me on Twitter. Yep, for just a few minutes, Jerry Colonna knew I existed and made time to interact with me. What a grown-up fangirl moment!

Like all good teachers, he used his words well. And like a good coach, he gave me something to think about and reflect on in relation to my own leadership.

His words of wisdom to me were: 'Broken-open hearts lead best.'

When Jerry talks about broken-open hearts, he's talking about peeling back the layers of yourself, to deepen your self-awareness, to understand that you are an imperfect human with all sorts of strengths and gifts and a whole lot of unhelpful behaviours, habits and thoughts. In his words, broken-open hearts belong to leaders who have done the work to unearth and to own what Jerry describes as the glory of you and the mess of you.

As leaders we can come face-to-face with our glory and our mess daily. And it's hard to stay with the discomfort of that. As humans we want to hide the mess or clean it up and just let the glory shine.

But we need glorious and messy leaders. We need imperfect humans who are okay with making mistakes. Glorious, messy leaders inspire and delight others by showing that being human is being authentic and being imperfect is perfectly acceptable. In fact, what if being imperfect is what makes you inspiring and relatable?

Grounded leadership is about understanding and leading yourself in order to understand and lead others. Doing the work of the Grounded Leadership Framework as a way to get to know and understand yourself makes you a better human. We need better humans as leaders. Doing the work of grounded leadership also means you are better positioned to understand and lead others with compassion and empathy.

But remember, not everyone shares the same knowledge and awareness as you, nor do they value or care about the same things. That doesn't make them 'wrong', nor does it mean you should shrink from meeting their expectations.

It does mean you will need courage to show up as the leader you aspire to be; to push your hair off your face and be seen and heard.

I hope you will.

I hope you'll back yourself.

I hope this book will nurture that little voice inside of you that says, 'What if I am already enough?'

I hope you'll see that what you experience internally – the stories, the nerves, the worry – is human. It's what humans experience – even the ones who look like they have it all together.

I hope you'll come to believe that you are enough; what you already have inside you to share is enough.

And, we need you to share it.

Leader, you don't have to be perfect. You don't have to wait until you feel ready.

You are ready to stand on your sacred ground – it will anchor and hold you, even when the ground shakes and things get choppy around you.

You are already enough. Now, leader, push the hair off your face and go.

THE GROUNDED LEADER'S GUIDE

- **G** Ground yourself in your values – stay anchored to what truly matters to you as a leader.
- **R** Reflect with curiosity – take time to understand how you are showing up, without judgement.
- **O** Open to growth – be willing to evolve your approach.
- **U** Understand your impact – recognise and seek feedback on how your leadership influences others, both positively and negatively.
- **N** Nurture connection – foster meaningful and high-quality relationships with your team, peers, students and community.
- **D** Decide with clarity – be clear on the leader you aspire to be and stay aligned with your vision and values.
- **E** Empower others – encourage autonomy. Believe in others and help them lead in their own right.
- **D** Delight in small wins – celebrate progress, and remember to focus on the gains ahead of the gaps.

REFERENCES

Achor, S. (2018). *Big potential: How transforming the pursuit of success raises our achievement, happiness, and well-being.* Currency.

Ahlers, A., & Arylo, C. (2015). *Reform your inner mean girl: 7 steps to stop bullying yourself and start loving yourself.* Beyond Words Publishing.

Bolte Taylor, J. (2008). *My stroke of insight: A brain scientist's personal journey.* Viking.

Brach, T. (2003). *Radical acceptance: Embracing your life with the heart of a Buddha.* Bantam.

Brown, B. (2012). *Daring greatly: How the courage to be vulnerable transforms the way we live, love, parent, and lead.* Gotham Books.

Brown, B. (2013, July 4). *The power of vulnerability* [Video]. RSA Replay. https://youtu.be/sXSjc-pbXk4

Brown, B. (2015). *Rising strong.* Spiegel & Grau.

Brown, B. (2018). *Dare to lead: Brave work. Tough conversations. Whole hearts.* Random House.

Collins, J. (2001). *Good to great: Why some companies make the leap... and others don't.* HarperBusiness.

Colonna, J. (2019). *Reboot: Leadership and the art of growing up.* HarperBusiness.

Dillard, A. (1989). *The writing life.* Harper & Row.

Durham, M. (Host). (2023, January 26). *Authentic leadership & how to find sacred ground* (No. 71) [Audio podcast episode]. The School of Wellbeing. Open Mind Education. https://openmindeducation.com/episode71

Dutton, J. E. (2003). *Energize your workplace: How to create and sustain high-quality connections at work.* Jossey-Bass.

Eurich, T. (2018, January 4). *What self-awareness really is (and how to cultivate it).* Harvard Business Review. https://hbr.org/2018/01/what-self-awareness-really-is-and-how-to-cultivate-it

Falecki, D. (n.d.). *Teacher Wellbeing Chat Box Conversation Cards.* Teacher Wellbeing. https://www.teacher-wellbeing.com.au/

Fitzpatrick, D. (2024). *The AI Educator.* https://theaieducator.io

Gilbert, E. (Host). (2015–2016). *Magic lessons* [Audio podcast]. Panoply/Elizabeth Gilbert. https://www.elizabethgilbert.com/magic-lessons/

Goleman, D. (1995). *Emotional intelligence: Why it can matter more than IQ.* Bantam Books.

Gollwitzer, P. M. (1999). Implementation intentions: Strong effects of simple plans. *American Psychologist, 54*(7), 493–503.

Grenny, J., Patterson, K., Maxfield, D., McMillan, R., & Switzler, A. (2012). *Crucial conversations: Tools for talking when stakes are high.* McGraw-Hill.

Hougaard, R., & Carter, J. (2018). *The mind of the leader: How to lead yourself, your people, and your organization for extraordinary results.* Harvard Business Review Press.

Jung, C. G. (1959). *Aion: Researches into the phenomenology of the self* (R. F. C. Hull, Trans.). Princeton University Press. (Original work published 1951)

Landry, C. C. (2019, April 3). *Why emotional intelligence is important in leadership.* Harvard Business School Online. https://online.hbs.edu/blog/post/emotional-intelligence-in-leadership

Lynch, J. (2024, June 19). *The way of the champion: How to win each day* [Audio podcast episode]. In M. Gervais (Host), Finding Mastery. https://podcasts.apple.com/au/podcast/the-way-of-the-champion-how-to-win-each/id1025326955?i=1000659488943

McCrindle. (2023). *Seven disruptors impacting the future of education.* McCrindle Research. https://mccrindle.com.au/insights/blog/seven-disruptors-impacting-the-future-of-education/

McCrindle. (n.d.). *Top leadership styles: Today's ideal leader.* https://mccrindle.com.au/article/top-leadership-styles-todays-ideal-leader/

McGee, P. (n.d.). *Polly McGee.* https://www.pollymcgee.com/

McQuaid, M. (Host). (2020, February 7). *Is the pace of change burning your people out?* (No. 190) [Audio podcast episode]. In *Making Positive Psychology Work.* Michelle McQuaid. https://www.michellemcquaid.com/podcast/pace-change-burning-people-podcast-jon-berghoff/

Nagoski, E., & Nagoski, A. (2019). *Burnout: The secret to unlocking the stress cycle.* Ballantine Books.

Nonviolent Communication Training Center. (n.d.). *What is NVC?.* https://www.cnvc.org/

O'Donohue, J. (1997). *Anam cara: A book of Celtic wisdom.* HarperPerennial.

Palmer, P. J. (2000). *Let your life speak: Listening for the voice of vocation.* Jossey-Bass.

Palmer, P. J. (2004). *A hidden wholeness: The journey toward an undivided life.* Jossey-Bass.

Peterson, C., & Seligman, M. E. P. (2004). *Character strengths and virtues: A handbook and classification*. Oxford University Press.

Rich, A. (1978). Power. In *The dream of a common language: Poems 1974–1977*. W. W. Norton.

Riley, P., Marshall, L., & Arnold, B. (2024). *The 2024 Australian Principal Occupational Health, Safety and Wellbeing Survey: Final Report*. Institute for Positive Psychology and Education, Australian Catholic University. https://www.principalhealth.org/reports.php

Robinson, V., Hohepa, M., & Lloyd, C. (2009). *School leadership and student outcomes: Identifying what works and why (BES)*. Ministry of Education. https://www.educationcounts.govt.nz/publications/series/2515/60170

Rosenberg, M. B. (2003). *Nonviolent communication: A language of life*. PuddleDancer Press.

Salovey, P., & Mayer, J. D. (1990). *Emotional intelligence. Imagination, Cognition and Personality, 9*(3), 185–211.

Schaffner, A.K. (2023.). *Understanding the circles of control, influence & concern*. https://positivepsychology.com/circles-of-influence/

Schwartz, S. H. (1992). *Universals in the content and structure of values: Theoretical advances and empirical tests in 20 countries*. In M. Zanna (Ed.), *Advances in Experimental Social Psychology* (Vol. 25, pp. 1–65). Academic Press.

Schwartz, S. H. (2012). An overview of the Schwartz theory of basic values. *Online Readings in Psychology and Culture, 2*(1), 11.

Schwartz, S. H. (2022, May 10). *Understanding values: The Schwartz theory of basic values*. Integration and Implementation Insights. https://i2insights.org/2022/05/10/schwartz-theory-of-basic-values/

Senge, P. M., Scharmer, O. C., Jaworski, J., & Flowers, B. S. (2004). *Presence: Human purpose and the field of the future*. SoL/Random House.

Siegel, D. J., & Bryson, T. P. (2011). *The whole-brain child: 12 revolutionary strategies to nurture your child's developing mind*. Bantam.

Sinek, S. (2019). *The infinite game*. Portfolio/Penguin.

Sinek, S. (2025, March 10). *You don't need your own vision – find one you believe in* [Video]. YouTube. https://www.youtube.com/watch?v=QGNgVu-i9bI

Strayed, C. (2012). *Wild: From lost to found on the Pacific Crest Trail*. Vintage.

Sullivan, D., & Hardy, B. (2021). *The gap and the gain: The high achievers' guide to happiness, confidence, and success*. Hay House Inc.

Taleb, N. N. (2012). *Antifragile: Things that gain from disorder*. Random House.

Vergano, D. (2023, October 25). *Divers in Mexico's underwater caves get a glimpse of rarely seen artifacts, fossils, and human remains*. Smithsonian Magazine. https://www.smithsonianmag.com/travel/divers-in-mexicos-underwater-caves-get-a-glimpse-of-rarely-seen-artifacts-fossils-and-human-remains-180985159/

Western Australian Museum. (n.d.). *Water in an arid land: Gnamma holes.* https://museum.wa.gov.au/explore/wa-goldfields/water-arid-land/gnamma-holes

Wheatley, M. (2023). *Who do we choose to be? Facing reality, claiming leadership, restoring sanity.* Berrett-Koehler.

Whyte, D. (2008). *Start close in* [Poem]. Many Rivers Press.

Whyte, D. (2010, April 27). Being at the frontier of your identity [Audio podcast episode]. In T. Simon (Host), *Insights at the Edge.* Sounds True. https://resources.soundstrue.com/podcast/david-whyte-being-at-the-frontier-of-your-identity/

ACKNOWLEDGEMENTS

This might be the trickiest part of the whole book to write. It's where I get to thank, acknowledge and appreciate the people who helped this book make its way into your hands. But of course, I can't name everyone. This book has been forming and layering since I was a child – shaped not just by the people listed below, but by a wide and unseen network of influence. Fingerprints, spirit, and wisdom are woven into these pages – some known, some unknown, some long gone. There are people whose contributions I may never fully recognise, others who have asked not to be named, and still others whose stories and strength are stitched into this work in quiet, powerful ways. So, those named below represent just a few threads in the broader tapestry.

Firstly, it has to be Laurence – your courage and honesty help me build my sacred ground and challenge me to show up as the best human and leader I can be. And when it all goes wrong, it's your kindness, unwavering belief, ridiculous jokes and genuine love that ground me. Thank you for sustaining me in very practical ways throughout the writing of this book – understanding that I needed time (lots of time!), making me great coffee (getting the grind just right!) and countless bowls of excellent potato and leek soup – yours is definitely better than mine.

To Selena, who kicked it all off with 'You need to write a book.' And to Alicia, who heard that conversation and ran with it. Thank you for your coaching and encouragement – especially the final push I needed to hit 'send' on the manuscript.

To my colleagues in the wild and adventurous world of solo work – especially Trudy, Daniela, Selena, Ellen, Luke, Win and Kate – thank you for the solidarity, the laughs, the generous cheerleading, and the truth-telling.

To Brooke, who edited my words with patience (great patience!), clarity and care. You kept my voice and sentiment, and seemed to effortlessly make it so much better. I'm so glad you were the one to edit this book. Knowing you were doing so in one of my favourite places, surrounded by nature (and your chickens!), made me feel even more at ease.

To the leaders who have shared their stories, triumphs and challenges with me in our work together – thank you. Your courage to share insights, wonderings and vulnerabilities gave me permission to connect with my own – and to see them not as flaws or failures, but just part of being human. Our conversations, reflections, and real-talk moments helped me rise above my doubts and shape the Grounded Leadership Framework as an invitation to lead with humanity and heart. You won't see your names in this book, but your stories and wisdom are stitched through every chapter.

To Rita, Jane, Nella and Ange – thank you for making time to read and comment on the book in its early stages. Your honest, helpful feedback and encouragement gave me the confidence to keep going when I wasn't sure I could – or should.

To Rose – what a wise woman you are, a true elder, and one I'm honoured to know. Thank you.

To my Irish family, the O'Donnell's, thank you for always welcoming and encouraging me. And especially to Mrs O for offering me a space with the best view in the world to retreat and write and for sharing your own stories so generously.

To my dear friends who stayed close during the waves of Mum's illness and all that came with it – you were my sacred ground. And as friendship and life flow on through travels and first Sunday lunches, I'm so grateful for you all.

To Petrina, for walking beside me through it all with humour, patience and steadiness. We're in this together – just as we quietly suspect Joan and Shirley always hoped we would be.

To my family – thank you for being part of my story in all the quiet, foundational ways that can't be listed but are deeply felt. Evan, my brother, who has been there for me and with me for as long as I can remember. Cassie – who is perhaps the bravest and most grounded of us all. Lauren – for the gifts of 2020 and 2021, and everything they allowed us to become. Jac – who surprises, challenges, frustrates and delights me, often all at once – as only the youngest sibling can. To the fabulous individuals who are my nieces and nephews – each one of you is a leader in your own way. I am so proud of how you show up in this world – grounded in presence, love, compassion, fun, and strength.

To Dad – who has always worked so hard to be an anchor for us all.

And for Mum. Who is everywhere.

ABOUT THE AUTHOR

Katrina Bourke has spent more than 30 years in education, learning what it really means to lead – and how to keep showing up when things feel overwhelming. A former deputy principal, she understands just how relentless school leadership can be, and how easy it is to lose your footing in the spin of everyday demands.

Today, Katrina works with principals, deputies and middle leaders across Australia. Her Grounded Leadership Framework has grown from years of listening, reflecting and gently challenging others (and herself) to lead in a way that feels more human-centred. Her approach is rooted in calm, clarity and compassion – not quick fixes or silver bullets.

Leaders often describe her work as both affirming and transformative. Katrina doesn't offer magic answers – but she does hold space for people to feel seen, supported and reconnected with what matters. Her guidance helps leaders lead with integrity, even when the pressure is high.

Grounded is Katrina's first book – a practical, reflective and quietly hopeful guide for anyone who wants to lead with heart.

When she's not coaching, facilitating or speaking, you'll find her walking through the bush, floating in the ocean or curled up somewhere quiet, with a cup of coffee and time to read, write and reflect. She also loves hanging out at home with her favourite people and pets.

www.ingramcontent.com/pod-product-compliance
Lightning Source LLC
Chambersburg PA
CBHW052036070526
44584CB00016B/2060

Chronic Progressive